A HANDBOOK OF PARISH YOUTH WORK

OTHER MOWBRAY PARISH HANDBOOKS

A handbook of
PARISH YOUTH
WORK

by

CLIVE ANDREWS

*Vicar of St Augustine,
Honor Oak Park, London*

*Former Youth Adviser,
Diocese of Southwark*

**MOWBRAY
LONDON & OXFORD**

Copyright © Clive F. Andrews 1984

ISBN 0264 66973 8

First published 1984
by A. R. Mowbray & Co. Ltd,
Saint Thomas House, Becket Street,
Oxford, OX1 1SJ

British Library Cataloguing in Publication Data
Andrews, Clive
    A handbook of parish youth work.
    1. Church work with youth—Great Britain
    I. Title
    267'.6'0941   BV4447

    ISBN 0–264–66973–8

Photoset by Cotswold Typesetting Ltd, Gloucester
Printed in Great Britain by Billings & Sons Ltd, Worcester

Contents

Contents

To
my wife
DIANA

ACKNOWLEDGEMENTS

Thanks are due to the following for permission to quote from published sources:
The Controller of Her Majesty's Stationery Office, for extracts from *Experience and Participation, Report of the Review Group on the Youth Service in England*, 1982.
Michael Day of the Brunel Institute of Organization and Social Studies, for lists relating to staff selection from *Framework for the Recruitment, Training and Support of the Part-time Youth Worker*, 1982.
The National Youth Bureau, for passages from *The Politics of Youth Clubs*, Sidney Bunt and Ron Gargrave, 1980, and from *Youth in the Local Church*, Fred Milson, 1981.

Foreword

Recent research in one London Diocese has suggested that the average age of London congregations is 59 years. That figure alone points up the urgent importance of the subjects that Clive Andrews is tackling in this book.

The work of the Church is always an unfinished work, in the sense that it has to seek to bring the coming generation into allegiance to Christ. Yet how is this to be done at the present time? I am particularly glad that Clive has offered us an important section on resources. People will always be our chief resource and our chief need. I greatly hope that after reading this book more people, in our churches and elsewhere, will come forward to commit themselves to this key part of the Church's mission today.

+ Keith Kingston

Introduction

On any day of the week thousands of Christian men and women across the country are giving their time and energy to work with young people. The effectiveness of such a massive workforce must be as great as possible for two main reasons. First, the needs of young people, whether Church members or not, are as great as they have ever been, perhaps greater. In a sense it matters not whether they are black or white, rich or poor, advantaged or disadvantaged; the very fact of being young means they are at a particularly formative period of their lives. Along with parents, grandparents, teachers and politicians, youth workers have a special responsibility for their growth and development. Young people who attend clubs need skilled and sensitive adult workers; so too do the large number of adolescents who never go near organized provision. Such is the challenge for those whose work encompasses church-going and non church-going youth.

Second, the young within the family of the Church are often referred to as the Church of Tomorrow. So they might be. But a healthy attitude to them will only be present when they are thought of as part of the Church of Today. If they are not treated as the Church of Today there may be no Church tomorrow. This means their full involvement, within their degrees of maturity, with decision making, with worship and with other activities of the Christian community. And it requires their building up in the faith, not encouraged blindly to follow accepted dogma but free to 'ask, probe and discover the truth'.

This book attempts to give practical help to any Church member concerned about work with young people. It is not for the professionally trained expert – he will have the skill to write a better book of his own! Inevitably a certain amount of 'philosophy' surrounds the practical suggestions and hopefully gives the rationale of why things are done, and done in a certain way. It does not however explain every last detail about being a good youth worker. Circumstances vary so much that this would be impossible. It is hoped, however, that what is said will be adaptable to the position in most parishes. Even then, dip into the book and take only what seems appropriate and useful in your own situation. Every suggestion has been tried somewhere and found to be successful.

People interpret 'young people' in different ways. For the purposes of this book I think of young people as those between the ages of 11 and 21. This is in line with the priority age range adopted in *Experience and Participation* the 1982 report of the Department of Education and Science on the youth service in England. At least some of what is said here is just as applicable to work with other ages.

The past twenty years have seen major changes in youth work. Here I make an attempt to relate those changes to youth work in the Church, hoping that some readers at least will discover new ways of revitalizing their work with the young.

Some will find this book approaches youth work in a way very different from the one they know already. I can only ask that they consider carefully what is said, rather than reject it out of hand simply because it is different. The Church has a significant capacity of inhibiting change by clinging to old ways of thinking and doing things. In a world that changes so rapidly, it will be no benefit to the young who live in that world if the Church does not explore new possibilities.

My thanks go to the numerous people who have helped with the writing of this book: especially to my former colleague Gwen Rymer and my present colleague Val Khambatta for numerous comments on the manuscript. I owe an exceedingly great debt to Dorothy Hearn who has converted written chaos into ordered typing, and to my wife who has read and re-read it all and made so many useful suggestions. Her spelling is also considerably better than mine!

October 1983   CLIVE ANDREWS

Chapter 1

Young People and the Church Today

England Now

Two days before writing this chapter I visited a small Dorset town. As I walked into the newsagent's I noticed something had changed since my last visit. The whole of the back of the shop now housed a video library. Video shops are hardly new in cities and suburbs, and their rapid spread there, and now in the country, points to a significant change in entertainment habits. In times past, people of all ages went out to cinema, theatre, concert or dance hall for most of their entertainment. Now the entertainment comes to them, on radio, four television channels, video films and in video games. The same tendency to stay at home is demonstrated by, and partly caused by, the rise in the popularity of DIY. So although leisure time has increased with shorter working hours, longer holidays, more labour saving devices and, for some, unemployment, a tendency has developed to spend that time at home. This has important implications for the traditional club-based youth work run by churches.

In the 1930s and before, life for most people was hard. Medical treatment was costly, years would go past without so much as a day's holiday away from home. Domestic furnishings were of poor quality and luxuries were few. Then,

1

in the years immediately after the Second World War, most people's financial position improved dramatically. Carpets replaced lino; refrigerators and televisions were bought. A week or a fortnight's holiday became the norm and eventually those holidays were taken in Benidorm rather than Margate. Family cars became commonplace, and many families became mobile. The situation was summed up well in Harold Macmillan's famous phrase (significantly coined from an American electoral campaign), 'You've never had it so good'. The rising graph of personal wealth has levelled off since the mid-70s but the social revolution of the years after the Second World War has left its mark on society. A chief aim in life has become to raise or at least maintain one's standard of living, and coupled with this is a deep belief that individuals have a right to enjoy themselves, and that freedom to 'do one's own thing' is an inalienable right. On the other hand, Christianity insists that the poor have a demand on the finances of the rich, that higher aims exist than enjoying oneself, and that there are rules which restrict how people act. This has resulted in a deepening chasm between people and Church. Signs exist among some young people that the emphasis is beginning to change, but the philosophy outlined here still seems prevalent.

The riches enjoyed by the majority have, however, failed to reach all sections of society. Many millions are still below the poverty line. Of particular concern are the decaying inner-city areas where the population is becoming increasingly a sub-culture isolated from the rest of society. The result of poverty, bad housing and lack of employment is most obviously seen in eruptions of street violence, but is also to be found in escalating violent crime especially among young people, and in the destruction of family and community life. Less well publicized are the changes taking place in rural communities. Fewer jobs result in migration to the cities, cut backs in public transport lead to isolation, and lack of local opportunities for entertainment, work and shopping produce a general dissatisfaction in the young. Unlike their

predecessors of even a generation or two before, they have
had held before them on the television screen a world of
infinitely greater diversity.

England, never the abode of a single unadulterated race as
some naïvely think, has had such a significant number of
immigrants in the past few decades that it is foolish for
anyone not to heed the implications. England is now a multi-
racial society. At its best the Church has set an example of
tolerance and understanding of other cultures and faiths. It
has acknowledged how much can be learnt from such
cultures and fought against attempts to subsume them. It has
recognized that many so called 'immigrants' are in fact
second or third generation citizens. For the health of the
nation, and in recognition of man's equality before God, the
need for young people to understand and respect each other's
cultures is as necessary for those in rural villages where a
black or Asian face is never seen as it is for those of whatever
race resident in Brixton. Church youth work has a vital task
here.

Equally significant has been the changing role of women.
It is hard to believe that less than seventy years ago women
could not even vote. Yet despite strides towards equality,
women are still the exception in the senior posts of many
walks of life – the law, politics and industry, for example. The
Church of England, constrained by the admittedly sincerely
held theological beliefs of some members, has been unable to
set the kind of example that would attract widespread
approval. Equality of opportunity within the youth club and
church (at least among laity) can help to establish a pattern
of thinking in young people which will be integrated into
adult life. The Youth Service and the Christian community
can also help prepare for the pressures created in both men
and women by women's enhanced opportunities.

Another well-publicized feature of late twentieth century
society is the high incidence of marital breakdown. Ease of
divorce may lessen the effort employed to make a relationship work, and greater financial independence for women

means less necessity to maintain a relationship at all costs. More positively, for some divorce has doubtless provided release from the destructive pain that had to be endured for ever in an earlier age, and slowly the Church of England is seeing that full compassion and forgiveness are not incompatible with theological ideals. But much has still to be done to prepare the young for marriage and to care for those scared by their parents' separation. Here again are vital tasks for both church and youth club.

Unemployment can have a destructive effect on the young. It is forecast that soon there will be no real jobs at all for the under-eighteens. The benefits brought to industry by the micro-chip revolution are counteracted by the human casualties. The Youth Service is beginning to respond to the needs of the young unemployed by, for example, opening premises during the daytime, advising on job applications, and encouraging an attitude which recognizes that human life has value even without paid employment.

The latter half of the twentieth century is also a time during which there has been a growth in government authority with little evident resistance by ordinary people. Openness about sexual matters, an increase in alcoholism, especially among young males, and a lack of leadership figures are other significant features. And hanging like a cloud over all else has been the threat of nuclear war. Seen by some as the chief reason for peace in Europe during the past few decades, and by others as a threat to be removed at all cost, it has inevitably been the subject of much heated debate and action not least among the young.

The Generation Gap
A rapidly changed and changing society leads many adults to conclude that young people today must be very different from the type of person they were in their own youth. This results in suspicion and fear, and stops some adults working with the young. But the division between generations is not

new. Try reading the following quotation to a friend and ask him to guess when it was first said:

'The world is passing through troubled times. The young people of today think of nothing but themselves. They have no reverence for parents or old age; they are impatient of all restraint; they talk as if they alone knew everything, and what passes for wisdom with us is foolishness with them. As for girls, they are foolish and immodest and unwomanly in speech, behaviour and dress.'

It was in fact written by Peter the Hermit in 1274.

But while criticism of the young has been common throughout history, and today's environment is very different from that of the past, it is important to remember that the basic needs of young people remain unchanged. An 'experiment' I often do with church groups is as follows (adapted from *Experiments in Growth* by Betsy Caprio (Ave Maria Press, Notre Dame, Indiana), an extremely valuable source book, available in Britain). I give each a sheet of plain paper and ask them to draw across the centre of the sheet a 'life graph' for the first twenty years of their life. The basic 'graph' looks like this:

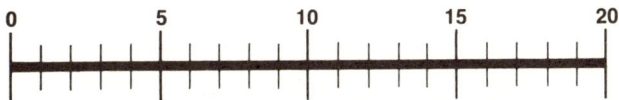

Next I ask them to plot on the graph their good and bad experiences. This may take a little time for recollection in the older ones! Participants must always be given 'permission' to leave things out if they do not wish to share them with the rest of the group. Crosses are placed *above* the line for good experiences, *below* the line for bad ones. The further above the line the better the experience; the further below the worse it was. Participants should try to remember how things felt at the time, rather than in retrospect. It is helpful, but not essential, to label the crosses. Eventually the graph will look something like this:

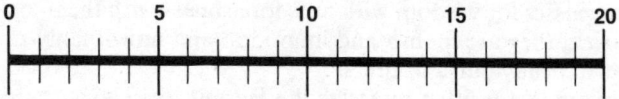

x got good job

x went to secondary
school

x confirmed

0   5   10   15   20

x broke arm

x new baby born

x left school –
missed friends

x parents went
abroad for 6 months

What is good for one may not be good for another. For example, going to secondary school can open up new horizons or can signal the start of bullying and lack of friends. When all have completed their graph, time is given to explaining the reasons for events being good or bad. (This can be done in pairs or small groups.) Useful discussion can follow, based on the results. Identifying the important, or otherwise, place of the Church can be valuable too. Almost always one general conclusion emerges. Life may be very different for young people today but basic needs remain the same: friendship, love, security, respect, self-esteem, just treatment. This is a useful exercise for any group of adults contemplating work with young people. It helps to break down the barriers age difference might suggest and leads to a sharpening of perception about young people's needs.

Features of Adolescence
Having noted the basic needs of young people, we need to examine more closely young people themselves.

Generalizations are all that is possible here, but generalizations are dangerous and no substitute for getting to know individual young people.

Certain features of adolescence are specially significant. First it is a time of rapid physical growth, in particular a time when a person becomes sexually developed, and is confronted by the strength of new sexual urges. Whilst some young people have a remarkable ability to view their sexuality rationally and to control it adequately, others find it dominates them. To some extent this depends on how open the family is about such matters, on peer group pressure, on how much they know about sex, and on their own particular libido.

Second, adolescence is marked by significant mental growth. The mind is particularly creative; thinking is exciting, but this can be dampened by the adult response 'be reasonable, be realistic'. Adolescence is also the first time a person considers not only what is, but what might be. The ability to look into the future and see alternative possibilities leads to choice, although young people never have total freedom from choice because pressure from parents, the Church, friends or whatever, narrows the field.

Third, adolescence is marked by a questioning of authority. For the first time young people begin to see that their parents are not always right. Neither for that matter are teachers, politicians or the clergy. Questioning of authority inevitably leads to conflict, though this can be creative as well as destructive.

Fourth, young people spend a lot of time contemplating themselves. They gaze into a mirror or appear to daydream endlessly. This is natural, for it is a time to learn about and understand the new self which is developing. Young people need space in which to get to know themselves. The sensitive adult can sometimes help too.

Facts and Figures
Few hard facts are available about the way young people

think and feel, but during preparation of the report *Experience and Participation* the Department of Education and Science surveyed over 600 young people (*Young People in the Eighties – A Survey* – HMSO). The findings are not so black as some would expect.

Of those surveyed 64 per cent thought relationships with the opposite sex should not become too serious. The majority saw themselves as friendly (84 per cent), responsible (73 per cent), and helpful (62 per cent); 67 per cent considered themselves to be contented and happy, while only 13 per cent said they were worried.

Generally they objected to being treated as children, wanted freedom from adult responsibilities such as decision making and the care of others, but welcomed freedom to act as they wished (and this necessitated sufficient money). In their leisure time their prime aim was to enjoy themselves. Most emphasized the importance of supportive parents, and looked to them for a pattern of what an adult should be.

The Church and Young People

Why does the Church fail to keep its children as they grow into their teens? Why does it not attract more young people? These are questions much on the minds of clergy and laity. A real concern is coupled with a sense of impotence and frustration.

Before examining reasons for non-attendance, one or two points are worth making. First, some young people at least have a very strong and mature faith and greatly value the contribution the Church makes to their lives. Second, the national picture of church attendance is perhaps not as grim as some imagine. *Prospects for Evangelism* (Bible Society, 1980) indicated that in England 8 per cent of the population is in the 15–19 age range, whereas 9 per cent of church-goers are in that age group. Only when the twenties are reached does church-going fall off. This age range constitutes 14 per cent of the total population but only 11 per cent of church-goers. These figures do not include the thousands of young people who attend church sponsored clubs. Third, some young people develop an awareness of God, explore aspects of Christian theology and attempt to live according to Christian morality, yet do not, at least at this stage in their lives, attend church. It would be dangerously wrong for the Church to dismiss them out of hand. An attempt to encourage church attendance may in some circumstances actually hinder their spiritual growth rather than aid it. Everyone likes to know how successful they are, and the presence of a person in a pew on Sunday morning is an easy and frequently used way of judging the success of a parish. It may, however, indicate no more than unthinking habit, and is a criterion which says little about depth of spiritual growth or perseverance in searching.

Despite what has been said, there is no cause for complacency. Materialism and a desire for freedom have already been mentioned as marks of society which set an ideological gulf between church and people. What else prevents the involvement of the young?

The language and customs of the Church can be a barrier, making it difficult for young people to feel 'at home'. Practices taken for granted by hardened church-goers can seem very strange to the uninitiated. Sitting in a freezing church early on Sunday morning, singing ancient words and music in an embarrassingly large and unconducive space, grown men walking around in long white 'frocks' – are just three examples of such oddities (nor is any of them *essential* to Christian belief and worship). Church language has a whole vocabulary of its own: surplice, psalter, aumbry, ASB, NEB, BCP. A full frontal has nothing to do with obscenity nor induction with child-birth. I am not arguing that such things should not be, but Christians must realize how strange it can all seem.

Like the Church sub-culture, there are youth sub-cultures too – punks, rockers, greasers, etc. They also have their own customs and language. Outsiders usually view them with some suspicion and fear. It should be no surprise if the

Church is seen similarly. This 'cultural' barrier must be overcome before new recruits feel at home.

Participation

Young people who attend churches are known to complain about the lack of opportunities which exist for them to be involved. Some, of course, prefer a passive role or have that demanded of them by external pressures such as homework and family commitments. But others feel moved to have a say in the running of 'the organization' and to participate in its activities.

The structure of parishes tends not to encourage involvement in decision making by the young. Few young people find a place on PCCs and if they do the nature and quality of discussion tends to dampen initial enthusiasm. Nor are they trained to understand the mechanics of committee work, or taught how to contribute to group discussion. Such training is necessary not only as initiation to parish decision making, but also as preparation for active Christian involvement within the community.

A useful way of ensuring that young people's voices are heard is to establish a parish youth forum. Here young people, with or without adult guidance according to their maturity, can air their views on both local and broader issues. Nothing, however, is more disheartening for young people than to spend time expressing their opinions if at the end of the day no adult seems prepared to listen or act on what they have said. Much of what is written later about members' committees in youth clubs is applicable here (see Chapter 3).

Under the parish umbrella can be found a wide variety of activities – bell-ringing, singing, cleaning, gardening, laundering of robes, running jumble sales, as well as reading, leading the intercessions, being members of committees, visiting, etc. If young people are expected only to participate in the mundane chores they may receive the impression that the adults think that is all they are fit for. Membership of the

Church means equal opportunity for all, whatever age, with the restrictions only of individual ability and personal volition.

Authority

In times gone by authority emanated from particular jobs or roles. A man had authority *because* he was a policeman, a teacher, or a clergyman. Such authority still exists to some extent as is shown by the uneasy feeling many people experience when talking to such a figure. But increasingly it is the quality of the man or woman that produces authority, not his or her job. So the unjust policeman is openly scorned, the class of a weak teacher is unruly, and the clergyman's message is judged on the quality of his life.

In line with this general change in society, the Church has lost much of its intrinsic authority. No longer is the Church listened to simply because it is the Church. Its arguments, like those of any other organization or person, are open to question and discussion. It must prove its worth and correctness in the open market. This is particularly true as far as young people are concerned. The day is past when the Church can successfully *tell* young people what to believe and how to act. Today is a time for sharing, exploring, testing and experiencing.

Knowledge

The Christian way of life cannot be explored, let alone followed, unless a person has some knowledge of it. Knowledge may come through reading the written word, hearing the spoken word or through experience of a Christian person or community.

In the past a main source of knowledge was religious teaching in schools and Sunday schools. Many non-church schools give Religious Education a lower priority than formerly, and a (correct) desire to do justice to our multi-faith society has resulted in less time spent on Christianity. One thirteen-year-old girl told me the four gospels were Matthew, Mark, *Luton*, John. This is not untypical of the level of knowledge one finds – a collection of half-learned and half-understood odds and ends, often coupled with magical overtones. Though it needs to be added that it is unfair for the Church to expect state schools to do its Christian education for it. The marked drop in numbers attending Sunday school is also significant: few have the opportunity to learn from this source. Nor do many young people attend church with their parents, so learning through experience of the Christian community happens only infrequently too. The Church needs to impart knowledge before it can expect commitment.

When I was a child ...

'When I was a child', wrote St Paul, 'my speech, my outlook, and my thoughts were all childish. When I grew up I had finished with childish things' (1 Cor. 13.11). Finishing with childish things is an important part of adolescence. It may show itself in turning to new interests and hobbies; new friends replacing old; a different attitude to school; and conflicts at home as the old child-parent relationship is hammered into something more approaching friendship or at least mutual adult tolerance. It is not surprising that if church is seen by a young person to be part of childhood then it too is finished with and replaced by some new activity and set of beliefs.

The aim of any parish should be to present new aspects of the Church to the young as they develop. Sunday school may be appropriate to children, but is there another activity for those ready to turn their backs on childish things? Or if organized activities do not appeal, has the parish addressed itself to other ways of maintaining a link between Church and young person? Or if the young person leaves the Church altogether, is there an attempt to make the parting such that the young person will find it easy to return (making him feel guilty about his departure is unlikely to help)?

Private and Confidential
Adolescence is the age of embarrassment. It has been said that embarrassment happens because people put over in public an image of themselves which is not totally true. It may be an image wholly different from reality, or it may just be a 'polished up' version of the real thing. Either way, if for any reason the mask slips, embarrassment follows. The adolescent is particularly susceptible. During adolescence each person has to decide which personal traits and desires he wants to emphasize and which to make subordinate, and which ideas will be allowed to govern his choice of career, friends, abode and partner. Part of this process involves trying out the roles. So, for example, a young person may experiment with a hard, unfeeling and capable image. Anything which happens to damage the temporary image will cause embarrassment.

Adolescents may also be embarrassed by the breaking of social rules. They have had little time to learn the laws of social interaction and so are more likely to contravene them unwittingly. They also have a great desire to appear grown-up, so infringing adult social rules is experienced as an open admission that they have not yet attained maturity.

Bearing this in mind, it is not surprising that many young people prefer to keep their religion private. Revealing to non-Christian friends an interest in things religious may result in considerable ridicule at a time when it is important to have the approval of one's peers. Even within the Church community it can be extremely embarrassing to reveal one's 'transitional' beliefs and doubts in public: those more experienced or intelligent could easily criticize, or point to flaws. It is not surprising then that young people tend to keep any interest in Christianity private and confidential. Going to church can itself be a great cause of embarrassment, for example if seen by a friend from school or work.

The ease with which adolescents can be embarrassed argues for a great sensitivity when dealing with them. After all, one way of overcoming embarrassment is to run away from whatever causes it.

Boring and Irrelevant

'Boring and irrelevant' is a phrase often used by the young in dismissing the Church. For some it is just an excuse for having nothing to do with it, for others it is a true reflection of past experience, while for others still the church impinges so little on their consciousness that they formulate not even such a disparaging opinion.

Those who see the Church as boring and irrelevant because of actual experience are likely to have had contact only with its liturgy and worship; after all this is the contact point for most people. And there is no denying that whilst the services in some churches are of a high quality, many strain the tolerance of adults let alone young people. But the majority of young people do not even have experience of its liturgy by which to judge the Church – no one has ever introduced them to it. Their judgement of the Church will probably depend on the quality of R.E. teaching in their school, and, as we have already seen, this too is inevitably of varying quality.

How then does the Church reach young people? How does it encourage initial thinking about Christianity, or dispel unfortunate conceptions? One way is to continue to work towards higher standards in public worship (especially in occasional services). There is no doubt this is necessary, but more profoundly the Church needs to go out to young people where they are with a message that can be seen as relevant: waiting for them to make the first move is not the answer.

If we look at the ministry of Jesus we see that he frequently taught and acted in a way particularly appropriate to those he was confronted with at the time. He symbolically multiplied loaves and fishes when surrounded by the hungry;

he spoke about the problems of wealth when face to face with a rich man; he changed water into wine when bad catering had left wedding guests thirsty, and he emphasized the status of children when disciples tried to send them away. Although he preached a gospel for all people of all generations, its proclamation was firmly rooted in the needs of the hearers. There is no reason to think it should be otherwise today.

I fear that to proclaim a message that begins with the goodness of God, life after death, and the forgiveness of sins is to start in a different world from the one inhabited by most young people. Their minds are not concerned with such eternal issues but rather with employment or unemployment, with having sufficient spending money, with relationships with parents, sexual relationships, with self-image and self-realization. A Church which starts where young people are stands a chance of being heeded. This suggests first that more attention should be given to understanding young people's needs and preoccupations. We will not form a relationship with them unless we understand them. Secondly, the highest priority should be given to those occasions when the paths of young people and the Church tend to cross anyway, and where there is a natural opportunity for the Church to show its love and concern – here I think particularly of marriage and baptism preparation, and also of crisis times when a young person might turn to the clergyman (or Christian club leader) for comfort and advice. Thirdly, it urges us to make known as widely as possible (in the local press for example and through personal contact) that Christianity has something to say about everyday issues like housing, employment, and the general quality of man's environment. If the Church shows an interest in their problems, they might just show an interest in Christianity.

Conclusion
Above are just some of the reasons why young people drift away from the Church or never come near it in the first place.

Much careful thought and hard work is needed if the Church is to share the gospel effectively with the young: the reward will be the knowledge that some young people at least have had their lives profoundly enriched.

If I were asked to sum up the relationship between young people and the Church, I would say that young people are more frequently wanted than loved. To love them is essential.

Chapter 2

Leadership and Styles of Work

Worker or Leader?

Does your church have 'youth workers' or 'youth leaders'? Almost certainly the choice of title will illustrate how the relationship between the adults and the young people is seen. 'Leader' implies someone who is out there in front and who is worth following. 'Worker' suggests someone who gets alongside young people. The Church needs more of the latter and less of the former. As someone has said, 'Leader suggests adults doing things for young people, more usefully we should be encouraging young people to do things for themselves – with the adults alongside to give help only when required'. One could say the same thing about young people and the way they think. It is far better that they explore the Truth for themselves with adult assistance when requested, rather than be the unthinking recipients of views and beliefs formulated for them by adults.

The People for the Job

First the clergy. It is doubtful if the incumbent of any parish has sufficient time to give to any one of the multitudinous facets of his job. He must be Jack-of-all-trades and perhaps master of only one or two. A long tradition associates youth work with the curate's role; assuming, with variable accuracy, that a 'youthful' leader is best at relating to youth. Human beings in the critically formative years of adolescence need great wisdom, understanding, patience, and resilience in those charged with their care. Few clergy beyond their time as curate have seen this as an area for specialization.

A decrease in the number of curates has put more work on the laity. Yet in a majority of parishes the search for volunteers, which is a massive endeavour for any task, takes on Herculean proportions when the work to be done is with young people. A myth expounds that a small 'elite' is good with young people, while the rest are not. Certainly some have instant rapport with adolescents, but that is not to say that they know how to exploit that relationship positively, nor does it mean that others cannot have their confidence boosted so they too can work effectively with the young.

Appointment

The selection of a new youth worker is frequently nothing more than a mixture of faith and luck. Faith certainly has a place in Christian youth work, but it is not here! And leaving things to luck is best avoided in all circumstances.

There are various traditional ways that workers are selected. First, an existing worker has a friend who would like to try his hand at youth work. He visits the club on one or two nights to see if he likes it, then by a process of 'seepage' he becomes part of the adult team. The vicar and congregation remain in ignorance of his existence for some time perhaps, and the young people eventually conclude he must be a new 'leader'. No-one has vetted him, no-one welcomed or inducted him. In the second alternative the vicar makes the initial move. He approaches a person of his own choice, quite possibly a day-school teacher (who would really like a break from young people in her leisure time). It is assumed that someone good in the classroom is effective in the youth club too. Youth work needs a different selection of skills from teaching and not all teachers are so equipped. But whether the person approached is a teacher or not, the vicar is making his approach on the basis of his own perception, and one person's view is more often wrong than the consensus view of a wider group. Further, the vicar may have made contact with the prospective worker without reference to existing workers. So, when the vicar arrives one night with the new volunteer in tow, the present staff are hardly in a position to say whether the new recruit is acceptable to them or not.

Now a better way of selecting personnel: first, advertise the vacancy as widely as possible. If you want a committed Christian then make sure the need is known by all the local congregation; announce it imaginatively in church, write about it in the parish magazine. Even if you end up making a personal approach, nobody can complain they would have volunteered if only they had known about it. Ask not only for volunteers but also for suggestions. Next consult existing staff. Arrange an informal meeting with possible recruits so that the other workers have a chance to decide if the new person fits in with the team. Make it clear to the new volunteer as early as possible that he is not guaranteed the job even though he is volunteering. It is better to risk upsetting him than to destroy a good youth work team and to halt the effective work it is doing. The management committee or support group should also be given the chance to express a view on the new appointment.

If – wonder upon wonder – more than one person volunteers for a vacancy, instigate a proper selection process. Holding selection interviews for volunteers is an uncommon practice in the Church, in youth work as well as in other fields. The majority of clergy are still appointed by the unsatisfactory 'word of mouth recommendation', so it is hardly surprising that a selection process is rarely used to choose volunteers. To select the first person to put his name forward is not a logical way of finding the best person for a job. In the end you may feel you can offer useful jobs to more than one 'applicant' but still we owe it to the young people to ensure that the unsuitable worker, however willing, is weeded out before he damages the work. At the selection interview consideration should be given to the following:

(a) Motivation   (c) Attitudes   (e) Skills
(b) Aptitudes   (d) Knowledge   (f) Awareness[1]

Further, wherever possible, staff teams should be balanced to take account of age, ethnicity, experience, occupation, sex and skills.[2]

Induction

Once appointed, how is the new worker inducted to the job? Commonly he is pushed in at the deep end with the hope (supported perhaps by prayer) that he will swim. Instead a carefully devised programme of initiation needs to be worked out even before the appointment is made.

Someone should have overall responsibility for the induction process: the chairman of the youth management committee or the senior youth worker. The function of the process should be to help the new arrival fit into the work as rapidly and successfully as possible. He will need to get to know the other workers (no worker should ever work alone, however small the group of young people). He will need help to learn the names of the young people, and he must be introduced to them as the new worker so that his role is quite clear from the start. If the new appointee is to work in a club then he will need to know the nuts and bolts of running it. Who, for example, holds the keys and what are the arrangements for opening and closing the premises each time? What rules are there? – it is best these are known before the young people start taking advantage of his ignorance! He must know what to do in case of accidents, where the nearest telephone is and what the agreed procedure is for dealing with injuries or sickness.

The new worker will also be better at the job if he has the opportunity early on to meet others in similar work. A visit to another club nearby could produce new ideas and would be particularly valuable to someone who is to have a senior position in a club. If the club is registered with a local authority education department (see Appendix 2), then the worker should be introduced to the local youth officer. Where the youth club is 'fed' from a junior club it is essential that workers have the opportunity to get to know the adults working with the younger age range and to visit their club. Many local education authorities and local voluntary groups periodically run induction courses for new workers. Someone without previous experience would benefit greatly from attending one.

Finally, time should be set aside after a few weeks so that the new worker and others involved with his work can assess how things are going. It is good practice to make all appointments for an initial period of, say, three months so that there is an opportunity for a graceful departure if the appointment has not been successful.

One final but important note: you cannot properly select someone for a job unless you know exactly what the job is. Most tasks within the Church have no written job description. In consequence they may be shaped by the personal inclinations of the people doing them, without regard to the needs of the situation. This is as true of most incumbents as it is of volunteer laity. Obviously a degree of flexibility is desirable so that the worker can use his own skills to the best advantage but there must be a broad framework which gives direction and parameters to the job. In the case of youth work the writing of the job description should involve the incumbent, the youth management committee or support group and any existing workers. It should also be referred to the PCC for their approval; even if this is a formality it encourages concern and support for youth work and those involved in it.

Parish Policy

Even the best youth worker can have the effectiveness of his work diminished if sufficient support of the right kind is not present in the parish. Three suggestions may help:

1. *Youth work should be reviewed annually, as should the personnel*

Young people change rapidly; more rapidly than at any other time of life. What meets their needs today may be rejected as uninteresting and valueless tomorrow. This is a tendency more noticeable in girls than in boys. Members are prone to move in and out of groups as friendships change, and as school leaving age is reached. New members will bring new interests, old ones take with them established approaches. An inflexible youth group, unable to respond to the changing needs and interests of its members, is unlikely to succeed.

Some youth workers have voiced their feeling of being given a life sentence when agreeing to work in a church youth club. If they leave, the club will fold. An annual review gives the opportunity for departure or re-negotiation of terms. It could be better to close a club than to risk the damage caused by the young people coming into contact week by week with a disillusioned adult long since drained of inspiration. Too often the club is forgotten by the adult congregation once it is known to be safely in the hands of an uncomplaining adult. An annual review gives all concerned a chance to voice feelings and thoughts.

2. *The youth worker needs to be valued*

Rarely do the names of the youth workers appear in the published lists of parish personnel. They find no place alongside those of the parish worker, the churchwardens, the treasurer and the organist. Custody of the young people is at least as important as custody of the church building. Most workers with young people labour and seek no such reward, but lack of acknowledgement indicates the standing he or she has in the total work of the local church. The worker must be valued and feel he is valued.

3. *Every member has a part to play*

Not all church members will be called to work directly with the young, but all can show interest, support the work in their prayers and give towards the cost. Start by looking at the church accounts. What portion of available finance is allocated to work with children and young people? Is it really sufficient? Lack of funds can easily prohibit effective work. Young people who belong to clubs should be encouraged to raise at least some of their own finance, but the financial resources of many young people are even more limited than those of the average parish church. To be financially self-supporting is too high an ideal for most clubs. Where church support is insufficient the youth worker frequently dips into his own pocket to meet expenditure; subsequently the church assumes it is more supportive than it really is, and when the worker leaves calamity follows. Outreach work to young people who do not attend clubs or other organizations can never be self-supporting. Financial support alone is not enough but is usually an indication of the importance the church family attaches to its youth work.

Training
Here the myth 'you're either good with young people or you're not' rears its ugly head again. Traditionally most workers have been appointed without any training whatsoever. To them is entrusted the development, wellbeing and spiritual growth of numerous young people simply on the basis that they are themselves young, that they have had children, or that they could find no reasonable excuse to alleviate the guilt that would have followed a negative answer to the vicar's request.

In the Methodist Church no youth worker is appointed without first having done a short training course under the supervision of a tutor allocated to him by the district. And it is the tutor's job, in conjunction with the local church, to encourage the worker to continue his training once in post. Many are the skills required by a youth worker – understanding adolescent development; planning the programme; counselling the individual; learning about the help, financial and otherwise, available from local education authorities; dealing with moral questions posed by the young; bringing Christian insights into the club;

helping young people assume decision-making roles; finding resources – the list is endless.

So too are the training resources available. There are books to be read at home; courses organized by local authorities, often very much geared towards the worker in a one-night-a-week youth club; general courses; courses in specialist skills from counselling to canoeing; very basic courses for the beginner and university standard ones for the advanced practitioner; and courses organized by the Church itself. They need not involve an enormous time commitment or massive financial outlay, but they do require motivation and a real concern to do the best that is possible for young people. Even the most experienced part-time worker would benefit from regular in-service training. (Details of agencies offering training can be obtained from the Diocesan Youth Officer or the Local Education Authority.)

There is an increasing tendency amongst professional youth workers to commit themselves to on-going non-managerial supervision. This means that each worker finds a personal supervisor whom he sees regularly and who has no managerial responsibility for his work. The supervisor is someone who is or has been involved in similar work and understands the problems. The purpose of the supervision is to give support to the worker and to give him the opportunity to have some objective comments made about his work. A similar scheme for volunteers, either individually or as a group, would aid their effectiveness.

Styles of Work
The qualities required in a youth worker will vary according to the type of work undertaken and the exact role of a particular worker within it. As well as the more established forms of church youth work, a number of alternatives exist. Many churches maintain patterns of work that are no longer the most suitable. To experiment with one or two of the alternatives may be a way forward. The report *Experience and Participation*[3] draws attention to the wide variety of

activities provided for young people. The Church has yet to expand into many of the areas that are well established in secular-run youth work.

Clubs

Of the traditional work the club is by far the most common. Youth clubs began in the last century and were instigated by the clergy, by universities and public schools, and by professional men and their wives. They started at a time when the young working-class poor were at great risk. Clubs attempted to develop body, mind and spirit and to inculcate the kind of disciplined approach to life required in the adult world of employment or wifely duties. The principal club activities were recreational, with a strong middle and upper class emphasis in the kind of activities encouraged.

Despite the passing of over a century since the first clubs, the Church is still firmly wedded to a style of work similar to that used originally. In 1900 B. Paul Newman published a book *The Boys' Club in Theory and Practice*. Writing about the less capable leaders of church clubs he said: 'According to these excellent people, the ideal Boys' Club would consist of prayer-meetings and Bible-classes, with an occasional missionary talk as a treat; lotto, spellicans, draughts and bagatelle . . . for amusements; and, perhaps, magic-lantern views of the Holy Land as a dizzy climax.'[4] Replace lotto, spellicans, draughts and bagatelle with other activities of a fairly sober kind like table tennis, snooker, pool, and, well, draughts, and for magic-lantern substitute 'film' and we have a programme of events not dissimilar to that offered in many church clubs now. In fact some clubs probably have less variety.

Closed Clubs

By 'closed' clubs we mean those that are closed to all but church-going young people. It is quite legitimate for a church to want to provide facilities for its own young. Being a Christian is no easier today than it has ever been. The young in particular need the regular opportunity of meeting together with their peers of a like mind both to socialize and to learn more of the faith. These are two distinct aims for a closed club. Some concentrate on the social aspect, providing mainly or totally games, music and a chance for members to chat informally amongst themselves. Others see their aim as providing a forum in which learning and worship can take place in a way especially suited to the age group. The two are by no means exclusive but the balance should be determined in direct response to the need of the local group.

Some church members who provide only a closed club are known to develop guilt feelings about not supplying open facilities for all the young people in the neighbourhood. A proportion of these might well be doing more for the non-church-attenders, in which case the negative feelings of guilt will hopefully be the spur to more positive action, but it is essential that sufficient staff of the right kind are available. It is better to run a good small-scale club for the committed than to attempt more demanding open work as well if resources are limited. Many churches support second-rate open clubs out of a (commendable) sense of duty to the neighbourhood when their resources of time and skills would be better used in caring for the few young ones in the congregation. This is not to say that all closed groups will be small, but sadly not many churches can now boast a glut of committed young people.

The staff for closed clubs obviously require a level of commitment to Christianity which may not be essential in open work. Particularly in larger open clubs with paid staff it is frequently necessary to employ workers who are better at youth work than at being church members. The ideal is the person who scores well on both counts but such personnel are not always available. It seems right in open clubs, so long as there is sympathy with Christian teaching, to choose the person who is good with young people rather than the one who knows his doctrine but is incapable of working well with the young. But closed clubs are different. Especially if they aim to be a place where the young learn more of the faith by Bible study, discussion or whatever means, then adults will only be of help if they are relatively mature in their commitment. It is essential to have adults who relate to young people in a constructive way, who can fire their imaginations, be sensitive to their needs and counsel them in their troubles.

Open Clubs

The term 'open youth club' covers a multitude of diverse provision. At the one extreme is the small one-night-a-week club in a church hall, staffed by two or three volunteers; at the other the club that is open most nights of the week, perhaps during the daytime as well, and is staffed by a large number of adults, some of whom may be paid, and catering for perhaps two hundred or more people during the week. The variety of activities on offer will vary greatly. Small clubs may provide a social area with coffee and refreshments and perhaps one alternative activity; football one week, a film, a table-tennis competition or craft work the next. Large clubs will have a range of activities taking place simultaneously ranging from pool to photography and from cooking to carpentry. They too will inevitably have a social area. Whatever the size, the aim will be broadly to offer activities to any young people who wish to take part.

Social Education

Some workers see activities as an end in themselves, but inevitably through participation young people learn and develop skills that go beyond those actually required for the activity. For example, table-tennis needs a certain ability with bat and ball and provides some physical exertion. But the young person will also, and less obviously, develop social skills equally necessary in other circumstances – learning to wait one's turn; abiding by the rules; the consequence of being dishonest (in scoring); awareness of the needs of others (who want to use the table). This is very basic, but some young people find it hard to exist harmoniously in society because these skills, that others take for granted, are underdeveloped.

Alongside specific activities like table tennis, the club will offer other opportunities for 'social education'. A fuller explanation of the phrase 'social education' is necessary before going further. It is a common phrase amongst professional youth workers but it is defined in different ways. Basically it is about enabling a young person (1) to live to the fullest within society and (2) to know how to set about changing society where it is seen to be deficient. How can this be achieved? First by offering situations through which young people will learn by doing. 'The process is one which starts with experience and leads through reflection to further experience, such experience being . . . of the widest kind and essentially self-programmed.'[5] The key here is the largest possible variety of activities; for exercising the faculty of choice is crucial to human growth. But the choice of activities need not be limited to things that can be done within the confines of the club. Community service has a long history and is a well-tried way of broadening horizons and deepening understanding of the community in which one lives.

Further afield, young people may be encouraged to participate in exploratory trips to other parts of the country or to other countries. (Details of agencies offering such experience are given in Appendix 5.) Although community service and international visits by their nature take place outside clubs, it is often from within the club setting that initiative for such things arise and where they are organized.

Participation

Coupled with provision of a wide range of activities is the need for 'self-programming' – the process by which the young people themselves determine the activities of the club. Being an authoritarian structure, the Church tends to have produced a predominantly authoritarian style of club leadership in which the vicar, curate or lay adult alone determines the kind of activities that take place. We deal here with decision making within the club. It is equally important to ensure that young people participate within the decision making process of the Church as a whole, as was seen in Chapter 1.

Participation consists in letting the young people themselves decide what activities their club will offer. Translated into structures this necessitates a 'members' committee' or representative young people on the adult management group (see Chapter 3). In clubs with a membership of only the very young, the adult workers and 'managers' will inevitably contribute more ideas and have to do more of the work but in those with older members they should be given the greatest possible freedom for 'self-programming'. Only in this way will they learn how collective decisions are made and put into practice. Even failures – perhaps particularly failures – will be points of learning. Skills discovered and developed in this way have lasting value to the young people concerned.

The Good Club
To summarize the features of a good club, be it open or closed, I quote from the booklet *Youth in the Local Church.*[6]
'. . . a good youth group is marked by six features:
1. A warm, friendly, encouraging, personalized atmosphere. Members are likely to feel that here they are valued as human beings: not for their promise or special talents, but simply becuase they are people. This quality is rarely articulated, but is communicated non-verbally through the ambience of the group.
2. Self-government is pushed to the limits of feasibility. Members have a hand in running the show, share the power and decision-making, give their own meanings to the association. The group belongs to its members, not to the adult worker.
3. It contains a challenge to take up new interests, to develop

one's own loyalties and to expand one's experience. Adolescence is one of the watersheds of the human journey: it can be a kind of second birth. At this stage, the mind may be open to new ideas, and the heart to loyalties; the hands can learn skills, perhaps for the last time in this life. In a good youth group, many things are happening. You can't make a horse drink water if it doesn't want to: but you may be able to make sure that a bucket of water is around in case the horse is thirsty. In a good youth group, the members and the adult workers are tempted – but never compelled – to take up new interests.

4. There is an attentive adult ear if any member chooses to talk about a personal problem. The adult's function is to listen, not to pontificate. Conversely, young people want an honest opinion, not pats on the head. As always, respect informs our best relationships.

5. There are opportunities to share in community enterprises of service and reform. Ideally, some of these are for the youth group itself, whilst others are inter-generational. The age gap is bridged most successfully when moral and educational tasks, freely chosen, are shared by people of all ages.

6. It provides both fun and responsibility. It offers drama, ritual and routine, and searches constantly for the growth points of self-determination.'

To see youth work in terms of social education is to lift it from its Cinderella place within education to a level of paramount importance within the work of Church and society.

Alternatives to Clubs

Earlier I referred to the way the Church is over-firmly wedded to clubs which are the traditional form of youth work. This is not to say that clubs are no longer of use; far from it, but it must be remembered that only a small proportion of young people go to clubs regularly. The figure in 1968 was 15 per cent.[7] Most of the remaining 85 per cent visit a club of some description once or twice but do not attend regularly, presumably because they find clubs are not for them. It is unlikely the figures have improved since 1968. Still, however, the major part of available time and energy goes into clubs, whilst, for example, there remains a great need for more widespread counselling facilities for the young.

Another alternative to clubs goes by the name of 'detached' or 'project' work. This work is described as offering 'care and service to the young people of a defined neighbourhood through personal relationships with youth workers. The project is primarily outgoing to its clientele . . .' (*Project Work in the Inner London Youth Service*, p. 13 (ILEA, 1980)). In other words the work is not concerned with those *attached* to a youth club but with reaching young people, wherever they may be found, in parks, pubs, shopping centres, or in the street. (Project work differs from detached work in that there is a 'base' – club, advice centre, etc. – to which the young may come occasionally.)

Although the Albermarle Report as long ago as 1960 advocated such outreach work (and it was in existence in America long before then), the Church, with a few notable exceptions, has failed to take up the challenge. This is particularly strange since it has a long tradition of outreach work in other fields.

Some Christians when first told of detached work, interpret it as an evangelist exercise – a matter of preaching the gospel in the missionary setting of the local neighbourhood. This is reminiscent of the old chestnut from the days of pre-englightened foreign missions. The missionary, Bible in hand, stood preaching to the natives with no apparent success whatsoever. After hours of fruitless oratory in the scorching sun, a native guide whispered to him that he might be more successful if first he gave the natives something to eat. Pangs of hunger the natives could not ignore, and only when their physical need had been met did the missionary manage to impart some spiritual food. Much the same is true in today's social jungle. The effective starting point is with the personal needs of the 'clientele'. The story of Easter may be an irrelevance to a young person whose pressing concern for the past two years has been his own unemployment. Show him some active concern for his problem and he may also want to hear what you have to say on other matters. Indeed the very demonstration of care will be your first words of 'preaching'. Not every church will be in a position to undertake detached work but some could well find it the way of extending and improving their work with the young.

How does one set about detached work and what are the problems? The main feature of detached work is that its exact nature is determined by the needs of local young people. To a large extent the 'target group' will be the most disadvantaged young people in the area. Rarely is it possible to make contact with *all* the local young people: time and manpower are too limited. So effort has to be aimed at those in greatest need. Professional detached workers in a locality where such work has not taken place before spend a considerable time – often months – getting to know the area and the places frequented by the young, and in beginning to identify the individuals or group who are least touched by existing youth provision.

The next task is to start learning about them, how and what they think, what their interests are, what their needs are. As a youth adviser I am all too frequently asked by clergy and youth workers 'What do you think the young people would like?' My answer is invariably 'Don't ask me, ask the young people themselves'. It is easy to make wrong assumptions about young people's thoughts and feelings. Certainly no detached work should be developed without sounding out those who it is hoped will benefit from the work.

Then comes perhaps the most difficult stage: gaining their confidence. Those who believe it is possible to walk up to a young person for the first time on a street corner and help him with his profoundest problem need to think again. It may take many months of increasing involvement with an individual or group before any benefit comes from the relationship, if it comes at all. The process may begin with no more than a smile while passing in the street. Then it develops through a casual 'good morning' to a few words about the vagaries of the weather. Eventually the opportunity for longer conversation may emerge, perhaps at the counter of a local shop or the bar of the pub. (Most of my own detached work was done in a local off-licence on an estate where no pub had been built. Most of the young people visited it at least once in an evening.) Only when confidence is built is the worker likely to be asked for help or advice. Not until then will the worker be someone to whom the young person comes of his own accord when he has a problem. From this it will be seen that detached work requires a long-term commitment. Some full-time workers in this field move on after a couple of years, just when they are becoming most useful. An extended commitment is even more necessary when the worker is a part-timer able to give only one or two evenings a week, for the process of gaining confidence will take longer (and the 'client-group' inevitably be smaller).

There is no denying that this work is difficult: more arduous than club work. Not everyone will have the right personality or approach, or sufficient confidence. Not everyone will have the endurance to stay with such a long process without losing enthusiasm. There will be no set pattern to work to – this will develop as needs are identified. Some people just do not work well in this kind of situation. It is hard to quantify success; there is no register, for example, showing a steady increase in numbers. Women workers are likely to have special problems; they may be viewed with suspicion and be at risk if they enter a pub alone with the aim of making contact with young males. Constant support is necessary both from management committees and from fellow workers. The task is made harder by the perpetually changing scene. Young people's habits change with the seasons, and superimposed on that are the irregular variations due to no obvious cause. They congregate in the park in summer, in the pub or coffee bar in winter, but for no apparent reason the street which attracted many young people one month is empty and deserted the next. The same group is now to be found five or six roads away.

For those who are prepared to take up the challenge of detached work, what might be achieved? Possibly nothing. There is no guarantee that the worker will be able to help anyone, or at least more than a handful of young people. But the aim is to establish an in-depth relationship with a few rather than a superficial one with many. A young person may ask for information or advice (knowing about local facilities and agencies for young people is essential). Sometimes the worker must admit he is unable to help. He cannot, for example, find the young person a job, but he may be able to help with writing job applications or identifying firms which might have vacancies. Another role for the worker is to bring the needs of young people to the attention of other bodies, the local council for example. Some young people have great difficulty getting their thoughts and views across to authority figures and the worker's role is both to speak for them and to show them how to vocalize their views for themselves in a way that will bring about the appropriate and desired results.

The project worker may also find himself doing small group work. This might mean becoming accepted from time to time in an existing group and feeding new thoughts into their discussion. Alternatively, it might involve instigating a group, perhaps in his own home, of those who seem isolated and need to develop friendships and the ability to mix with others. He may liaise between a young person and his family (only with the young person's permission) where relationships have broken down. He may visit isolated young people he has come to know in their own homes.

Even for those suited to it, detached work is not easy but the rewards are great.

Chapter 3

Management Committees and Support Groups

Management committees or support groups are by and large an alien concept in church youth work. They usually exist only when the work is financed, at least in part, by the local education authority. A normal prerequisite of such funding is that an adult management committee oversees the work and its expenditure. Even then the committee can be a formality rather than a support to the work. In most parishes the parochial church council assumes the management role but inevitably this is a task for which it is not truly fitted, nor one for which sufficient time is available. In practice once or twice a year, perhaps only once, at the parish annual general meeting, the youth workers present a report on their work and a question or two is asked about why numbers in the club have grown, or more probably fallen, since last year. This is nothing more than a token gesture; is not really management, let alone support, and by giving a false sense that obligations have been met, is worse than useless.

Membership
In Chapter 2 the need for workers to be valued and

supported was emphasized. To provide this is a chief aim of management committees. Such committees should consist of people, mainly drawn from the local church and community, with an interest, if not expertise, in caring for the young. A place on the committee is not a pathway to status and power but a role of responsibility (PCC members also take note!). Members should be prepared to attend committee meetings regularly, and some at least should be able to give time to activities, such as fund-raising, outside the formal meetings. The size of the group is important; ten is probably the maximum for effective discussion. But a common problem is not limiting the number but finding sufficient people with the required skills to make a well-balanced committee. In some areas finding such people is extremely difficult, and it may be necessary to have the smallest of groups. More people are likely to make themselves available, however, as interest in youth activities grows within a particular Christian community and adult members begin to understand the nature and importance of the work.

The committee might include a representative from the PCC, the local beat policeman, a social worker who works in the locality, a teacher from a nearby school and a parent, as well as other interested parties from church and community. Committees for closed youth provision will be more church orientated but should not be so narrow as to lose sight of the wider needs of the young people. It is perhaps closed rather than open work which most frequently has to fend for itself without a support group. It is just as important that this kind of work is supported and motivated properly and that the staff, even if only the curate and two lay workers, are adequately cared for.

Management Committee or Support Group?
Some people would say there is little difference between a management committee and a support group but here I use the terms to differentiate between two distinct types of group.

By management committees I mean those that have a formal management function as, for example, where the maintenance of premises and deployment of considerable funds are involved. Support groups are less formal and without such massive executive functions. Having said that, the two act in very much the same way, and most of what is said here is applicable to both.

Management in Action
Whatever type of group, it needs to be clear about its own purpose and aims. The report *Experience and Participation* states that 'in general the Youth Service could be better managed'. It then outlines the four basic aspects of management: 'defining objectives, assigning roles, allocating resources and monitoring performance'.[1] Broadly these can be seen as the tasks of any management or support group.

Defining Objectives is essentially the first job. The group must know what the youth work for which it has responsibility is trying to do. Is it there to provide recreation, to teach the faith, to evangelize, to give young people a welcoming place away from home, to offer an information and advice service, a combination of some of these, or what? To which age range is it primarily committed? From which geographical area is it aiming to draw its members? What are the pressing needs of young people? Having answered those questions the committee must then determine how it will set about achieving its aim. The overall aim is broken down into more manageable and short-term objectives. If the aim is to provide a small one-night-a-week craft-orientated club for 13-16 year olds in a particular village, then one of the objectives might be to have a selection of at least four different activities on each night. A second could be to have a bi-monthly painting competition, and a third to have an annual parents' evening during which a display of work would be on show.

Assigning roles is next. Pursuing this particular example, who is to supervise the four activities each evening? Who is to be responsible for funds and who for fund-raising? Who will provide craft materials? Who will ensure repairs are done, and who will look after safety matters? If youth workers and committee members are not clearly allocated tasks, jobs tend to get left undone.

Next comes *allocation of resources*. Often this will mean the distribution of *money*. How much should be spent on craft materials; how much on occasional outings or staff training? Should pottery be introduced even though half the year's budget will go on a kiln? The allocation of resources could also be about manpower, or the way space and equipment are shared between activities.

Last comes *monitoring performance*. Having decided what to do, who will do it and how the resources should be used, it is easy to let the work run its own course for better or worse. Monitoring performance is essential if mistakes are not to be repeated. In the example here, the committee would want to assess the club. Had as many attended as had been expected? Were they enthusiastic? Was the club costing too much, and if so should activities be limited or fund-raising increased? Was the aim still good but some of the objectives in need of revision? Was the last parents' evening a disaster?

Occasional reference to these four aspects of management – defining objectives, assigning roles, allocating resources and monitoring performance – will help ensure that any committee with a management role is properly performing its function.

A committee must above all else ensure that the work of the club, advice centre, detached project or whatever, is done as successfully as possible. This can only happen if it has to hand all the necessary information on which to make well-informed decisions. In most situations it is the youth workers who have the monopoly on information: they are in day-to-day or week by week contact with the young people, with other staff, and with the building, if any, that is used for the work. It is essential therefore that management committees regularly receive full reports on what is happening and give the workers a chance to share their successes and problems. Supporting the workers is the chief way of supporting the work, although there may be times when the committee wishes to question the worker's action or, in extreme cases, even call for the removal of staff if they are standing in the way of effective work.

Buildings
Committees which have a dual role tend to find it more difficult to support work adequately. Most usually such committees have responsibility not only for youth work but also for the premises where it takes place. And more often than not the building is used for other gatherings as well as youth work. No church member needs reminding of how time-consuming buildings can be. What frequently happens on a dual-purpose committee is that consideration of youth work is pushed into second place behind endless discussion on repairing the flat roof, the difficulty of finding a cleaner and the need for added security. All such items are important but take time away from supporting the youth workers and their work. One solution is to separate the functions and allocate them to different groups. The problem then is to ensure good liaison between the two committees so that the needs of the young people are fully appreciated by those who run the building. A common core membership of both committees is essential but this naturally makes increased demands on the members and may be unacceptable. It is still the best solution where the premises are used by a number of groups and the use by young people is fairly small. The other solution is for the chairman to discipline himself and his committee so that adequate time is given to managing and supporting the youth work. But the majority of people find it easier to talk about buildings and this approach requires constant vigilance!

Members' Involvement
The membership of management committees and support

groups is of utmost importance. It has been said already that members should primarily be drawn from the local church and community: this is essential if the work is to meet the needs of local young people. It is even more important that the young people themselves can be heard at management level. There are two main ways of achieving this. Either a proportion of the seats on the committee are reserved for young people, or a separate 'members' committee' is set up with channels through which it can make its views heard by the adult group. If the main management committee is a formal body with legal responsibilities for property and funds then it will be impossible to have under-eighteen year old members with full membership. Such a committee is legally liable in certain respects and those under the age of majority cannot play a part. Young people under eighteen could be non-voting members but this is unsatisfactory as it only seems to emphasize in a negative fashion that they are in some way inferior and not yet mature enough to be fully responsible. The answer in this case is to have a members' committee, but it is important that they feel their decisions are listened to. No young person is going to give up his time to discuss the activities of his youth club if no action happens as a result. Members' committees must not be a token gesture but an essential part of informed management.

If it is possible for young people to be full members of the adult committee then they must be encouraged to contribute to discussion. Few young people find it easy to share their views in a predominantly adult group and a gentle rebuke by the chairman which would go almost unnoticed by an 'old hand' may put off a young person from ever contributing again. It is especially helpful, if there is a formal agenda, for the chairman or a member of the committee to go through the papers with the young people before the meeting so that they understand procedures and the topics to be discussed. One young person alone on a committee will be at a particular disadvantage: two or more, to give each other support, is best, and, if the committee is responsible for a club, then they should be elected by the full membership, so they can be as representative as possible.

Frequency of Meetings

The usefulness of a management group is determined to some extent by the frequency of its meetings. The supporting role that is at the heart of any youth management committee requires that members work well as a team and this in turn necessitates regular meetings. As much as anyone I deplore time wasted on unnecessary gatherings, but if a management committee or support group is really to keep abreast of the work for which it has responsibility and actively support the workers, then frequent short meetings are much to be preferred to lengthy ones so far apart that much of the time is spent refreshing memories about what happened last time and rebuilding effective member relationships.

Another way of cementing a committee together and so aiding its usefulness is to hold an occasional social event for it and the workers. In addition, much can be said informally over a glass of wine that would be suppressed in a more formal meeting. Such a social gathering is especially good when a new committee is formed and members are strangers to each other.

Training

However much members have to offer on their appointment, virtually all would benefit from some kind of training. Training for committee members is the most neglected area of youth work training both in the voluntary and statutory sectors. General training in management or in youth work itself would be important to all members, except those already well versed in the subjects. Some may wish to go further and learn more about a specialist area such as the problems of drug and solvent abuse, working with girls, or counselling. Some local education authorities and dioceses offer suitable courses or training days, as do other voluntary groups. Where nothing is already available it could be that an organization will respond to pressure and put on an event.

Some management committees have found it valuable to spend an evening or a whole day with a consultant/trainer. The diocesan youth officer, an LEA youth officer or some other person experienced in the management of youth work could be used to make objective criticism of the committee's working and to suggest better ways of fulfilling its role.

Conduct of Meetings

Inviting someone to sit on a church committee could on occasions be a splendid form of punishment for the wrongdoer. Many committees would lose their tedious pointlessness if they were more structured and disciplined, and if members prepared thoroughly in advance.

Members should know well beforehand when and where meetings are to be held, and last minute changes in arrangements, if absolutely necessary, should be communicated to everyone. I recently drove over one hundred miles to a meeting only to find I was the one person they had forgotten to notify about the cancellation.

Agendas should be available in good time, together with any supplementary papers that members should read. It wastes everybody's time if long pauses have to be left while documents are read at the meeting. The agenda itself should include sufficient information so that it is perfectly clear what is to be discussed. 'Item 5 – Redecoration' just is not enough. One person will arrive expecting to discuss redecoration of the hall, another thinks the item is about the kitchen, another expects it will give him the opportunity to complain about the way young people deface the walls, and the treasurer comes prepared with figures to show that they cannot afford to redecorate the lavatories until next year. They all realize they have wasted time and effort when the chairman announces that the item is about whether some of the youth club will help redecorate the church.

Meetings should start promptly, and the place for

important topics is at the beginning of the agenda while minds are fresh and before members start drifting away, though a known finishing time will alleviate this latter problem. No meeting should last more than two hours. Detailed discussion is best left to smaller subcommittees which then report back to the main body. Minutes of meetings should be circulated as soon as possible so that those members who have 'been volunteered' to do specific pieces of work are reminded in plenty of time. Minutes should be sufficiently detailed so that at the next meeting, perhaps a month or so later, the recorded decisions are still perfectly clear. They are, however, minutes and not verbatim reports like Hansard.

The chairman's role is crucial. It is his or her job to move on discussion as rapidly and smoothly as possible, to ensure members keep to the point, to keep the talkative under control, and to encourage the shy. The meeting is not a passive audience for the chairman's monologue: he or she should encourage all to contribute, for those who cannot make themselves heard will soon lose interest. In between meetings the chairman maintains regular contact with the youth workers, and takes decisions which just cannot wait until the next full meeting.

Chapter 4

Running a Club

Clubs are without doubt the mainstay of the Church's provision for young people. In Chapter 2 the different types of clubs were explored – open clubs, closed ones, one-night-a-week clubs and those open most nights, and perhaps days, of the week. It was also noted that the widest possible range of activities is essential if young people are to benefit to the full, and that it is important to involve members in determining the programme. Chapter 3 emphasized the importance of good management, so that resources of time, money and personnel are used to the fullest advantage. Against this background we can explore running a club in more detail.

Closed clubs are dealt with specifically in Chapter 6: here we concentrate on one-night-a-week open clubs. Nevertheless much of what is said here could be modified to apply in other situations.

The ultimate aim of Christian youth work of whatever kind is to proclaim the gospel, but it must be recognized that this might rarely take the form of preaching and teaching in the conventional sense. Most likely it will involve identifying and meeting the immediate needs of young people; showing that the Christian community cares for them; and encouraging them to live their lives to the full.

Within the overall 'evangelistic' aim, each church youth club needs to set specific aims relevant to the young people it hopes to provide for. These aims should be determined and agreed on by both workers and management committee, and should be reviewed from time to time – say annually – to see if they are still appropriate.

Aims should be in broad terms yet precise. The aim might be something like: 'to provide recreational facilities for young people on the estate', or 'to enable young people of the village learn more about society', or 'to enable school age young people to develop into mature, thinking citizens'. This will be determined not only by the interests of the workers but by the needs of the young people in the catchment area.

Once the aim is established this can be broken down into manageable objectives. For example, if the aim is 'to help young people of the village learn more about society', then the objectives might be as follows:

1. To provide regular opportunities for members to talk together informally. If they are to learn about society, what better place to start than with each other. Informal conversation week by week will ensure a broader vision of how other people live.

2. To bring into the club from time to time visitors who have particular roles in the local community – the PC (in some inner city areas relations with the police have reached such a low ebb that the presence of an officer in a club can produce extremely strong adverse reaction), the vicar, the head-teacher of the village school, a farmer, a parish councillor, a magistrate. All these will have something to contribute to the stock of knowledge each young person has about society.

3. To have a film and discussion once every three months about a social problem such as drug abuse, homelessness or racial prejudice.

4. To have an outing once in six months to a place of interest; to a factory in the next town, to an air–sea rescue station, to London or another big city to look perhaps at the different kinds of housing that can be found in just one small area. All these need imaginative handling. The club meeting before the visit could lay the foundations by identifying things

to look for, and the one after could be used for a review of how members felt and thought, and for a sharing of new knowledge gained.

5. To ensure that posters showing major social issues are on display in the club week by week and that they are changed regularly.

The sixth objective might be simply to have a good programme of recreational events interspersing the other items, so that interest is maintained and fellowship fostered, and the whole thing is as enjoyable as possible. Without an element of enjoyment it is difficult for anyone to learn anything.

An established pattern of activities should not become sacrosanct. Unsuccessful events should be noted and removed from the programme if beyond improvement, and new ideas, including those of the members themselves, fed in.

Premises

Good buildings do not in themselves create good youth work, but bad premises can annihilate it. Everyone knows how one can feel relaxed and at home in one person's sitting room, and ill at ease and uncomfortable in another's. That may be due in part to the reception given by the owner whose home it is, but it will also be because of the decor, the furniture, the lighting and the state of repair and cleanliness. Club premises affect young people in the same way. No young person is going to be uplifted by, or attracted to, a large Victorian hall lit by yards of white fluorescent lamps, insufficiently heated, and decorated in drab greens and browns, dirty, and in a dubious state of repair. Yet all too often this is the very kind of building in which clubs are held.

Dealing with each aspect in turn, it is not over difficult, nor costly, to improve premises. The barn-like proportions can be broken up by the use of portable screens. (I say *portable* screens because most halls will be used for other activities as well.) The young people themselves may be able to construct suitable screens from light timber frames faced with hard-board, cardboard or material, and decorated with magazine pictures or paint. Alternatively, two or three adult members of the congregation may take on the construction job. The screens need firm bases to ensure they stay upright and to avoid accidents, but they need only be about six feet high and reach nowhere near the ceiling or rafters, but will have the effect of breaking up the area into more 'human' space. They can be used to create a lounge area, to screen off the canteen, or to separate one activity from another. As a temporary measure until screens are made, tables positioned end to end or rows of chairs might be used to divide the space; not so effective but better than nothing.

Lighting is of utmost importance. Bright overall lighting will be needed for football, basketball and similar games, but most other activities do better with more subdued or directional lighting. If the services of a competent electrician can be found among the older membership, or again, in the congregation, then it will not cost a lot to install a basic secondary lighting circuit. The lounge area and canteen would benefit from quite a low level of light, so long as it is not so dim as to be dangerous. Here coloured and/or white light might be used, and an old table lamp or standard lamp could be made use of. Table tennis, pool, and similar games are effectively lit by a couple of directional spotlights. These give good light but also create a 'pool' round the games area, which psychologically sets it apart from other areas.

The overall decor may be a more difficult problem. Scaffolding might be necessary in order to paint the ceiling and hiring it is expensive, the quantity of paint needed might in itself be a large budget item, and as the hall will almost certainly be used by other groups and not be owned by the club, a decision to redecorate will rest elsewhere. Some churches have been able to use young people on a government training scheme to do this kind of work. If the body that owns and manages the hall cannot be persuaded to redecorate, either because funds are not available or because commitment to youth work is too small, some improvements can be made in other ways. Club members could paint a mural on one of the walls, perhaps of a local view, or if this is unacceptable, then the picture can be painted on an old sheet and used as a wall-hanging put up only when the club is in session. Another alternative is to use posters available from any number of sources. Notice boards can serve a similar purpose as well as being a repository for odds and ends of information.

Furniture is another aspect of the club's ambience that may not be totally within the club's control. The use of the hall made by other groups may limit the amount of equipment and special furniture the club can store. If possible at least a small area should be set aside with comfortable chairs and low tables where young people can sit and chat or play cards or board games. Suitable furniture might be available from one of a number of charitable sources. Large firms regularly replace their furniture and fittings and will donate redundant items to clubs if transport is arranged. Firms with a number of retail outlets may have a depot for furniture: the manager of a branch should be able to supply the address. It is no use, as one naïve professional worker did recently, going into your bank and asking the cashier if she has any furniture she doesn't want! From shops, banks and other businesses I have known clubs get, free of charge and in good condition, chairs, armchairs, tables, carpet tiles, notice boards, room dividers, paint, curtaining, and more besides. Furniture should be of reasonable quality and not ancient unsaleable items from the parish jumble sale. You are not equipping a five-star hotel but you are trying to create an attractive environment young people will look forward to visiting.

For the same reason repairs and cleanliness are important. An evening spent in a hall made freezing by cold air blowing through broken window panes is not an attractive prospect. Neither is buying drinks and sweets from a canteen which is dirty and squalid. Once again these things may be outside the direct control of the club's workers and managers, but in that case pressure must be put on the PCC or whoever has responsibility for the building. Offering to do repairs, or ensuring that the hall is tidied at the end of club night, may also prick a few consciences.

Despite the above it is possible to make club premises so nice that young people feel ill at ease. On the other hand a tatty club produces a tatty attitude towards it. If furniture is slightly damaged it is asking to be damaged further unless repairs are made at once. Likewise one word of graffiti on the walls is an open invitation to treat them as a blackboard. And one piece of litter on the floor makes the whole area a potential litter bin. Proper litter bins – or cardboard boxes – are essential, especially if there is a canteen.

Finance
Like buildings, ample finance does not make good youth work, but lack of funds can destroy the possibility of effective work and demoralize the best of workers. It has been said elsewhere that the amount of finance made available for youth work is some indication of what priority a church gives it. But unless there are mitigating circumstances (for example a disabled club or one for young children) the membership should raise some of their own funds.

Views vary about 'subs'. Some would argue that, especially in deprived areas, it is too much to expect young people, the unemployed, for example, to pay each time they attend. I lean towards the opposite view that, so long as 'subs' are not prohibitively high, payment for attendance creates greater loyalty and a respect for the premises and equipment. Exceptions can always be made if the worker knows a young person or his parents would find the payment difficult. This should be a private arrangment between worker and member and on no account should the young person be subjected to his 'charitable status' being broadcast to all and sundry. The worker needs to be firm, however, with those who falsely plead poverty.

A well run canteen can also make a small profit for the club which can be channelled into other activities. Canteens that make a loss are either badly run or the takings are being purloined.

Finances can be supplemented from time to time by the organization of fund-raising events. Almost anything can be sponsored, from swimming through walks and football matches to singing and collecting waste paper. Jumble sales or sales of work are popular, as are raffles and car washing. Whatever form of fund-raising is chosen the most successful are those that the members themselves have opted for. They are unlikely to give an event wholehearted support if only the workers and the vicar are really keen on the idea. It is best to involve the members from the beginning by convening a small committee to master-mind the whole project. Raffles and collections present problems. The law regarding them is detailed and precise. Before undertaking either, contact the police or someone who has experience of such things to ensure that all requirements are met.[1]

Charities are another source of income. Some are overburdened with requests, but experience indicates that many have more money than they know what to do with. The problem is finding out about them in the first place, and then knowing how to approach them in the right way. A local library should be able to provide a copy of the *Directory of Grant-Making Trusts* which gives details of large and small charities alike, classified in areas of concern, and this is the best starting point. It takes some hours to wade through the pages of entries but this is essential if the most appropriate charities are to be unearthed. Alternatively the local education authority or youth office may know of local educational charities, or there could be parochial ones known to the incumbent.

Most, perhaps all, charities will not pay for running expenses but will consider contributing towards major items of expenditure such as new table tennis tables, a small trampoline or new kitchen equipment, or will fund a summer holiday, or a weekend away for club members. It is worth being bold with one's application. Asking for money for two or three packs of cards is unlikely to warrant the time it takes to process the application; a request for a whole range of board games is more reasonable. After all, the charity can always reply that they will provide for only a proportion of the goods required.

When writing to a charity give sufficient details but do not overburden them with information which they really have not time to read. Give details of your organization, what it does, where it meets, how many it caters for, etc. State specifically what you need money for and include an accurate figure for the total cost (better to give the whole amount and see how much they will donate, rather than only ask for a percentage in the first place). Above all show that you are making an effort to raise some of the money yourself through accumulated subs, a jumble sale, or whatever. Charities tend to respond best where their contribution will encourage others to work harder for themselves.

In some circumstances there may be only one charity you can approach which seems to fit the bill. If there are a number, pick say half a dozen and make an initial approach giving the sort of details outlined above. From some you may hear nothing, others will politely refuse because you don't meet their criteria, some will send a formal application form or request specific details, a few will act on the information you have originally supplied. If all the first half dozen decline to help, select some more. Despite the expense with ever rising postal charges, it is well worth enclosing a stamped addressed envelope for your reply. Be sure to write and thank charities which help you. Leaving pure courtesy aside, you may need to apply to them again.

Insurance

Just two weeks before writing this my wife and I returned from a night away from home to find we had been burgled. Although the losses were greatest at the sentimental level, it was good to know that insurance would at least make good the financial loss. It is easy to be blasé about insurance. Usually years go by with no need to make a claim, but incidents like that above remind one of the need for insurance, and adequate insurance at that. And in a club it is not just insurance against theft that is required.

Perhaps most important of all is *Public Liability* or *Third Party Insurance*. It is not unknown for someone using club premises to be injured through the negligence of the management committee. Even if the club is not found liable in a particular instance, the cost of defending a legal case can be very considerable, incurring expense well beyond the means of any club. Where liability is proved, compensation can run to tens of thousands of pounds.

In certain circumstances individual members of a management committee can be held responsible for paying damages in addition to the club itself, so it is essential that no club is without Public Liability Insurance. Before arranging such cover, clubs should investigate whether the policy held by the church (or other organizing body) already covers them.

Not all accidents, of course, happen because someone has been negligent. Pure accidents occur in even the best run clubs. *Personal Accident Insurance* provides a scale of payments to the injured person according to the severity of the injury, or a payment to relatives in the event of death. No legal compulsion exists to provide such cover but most clubs feel a moral obligation to ensure that should an accident take place some financial assistance can be provided to help with medical and other expenses. It is especially valuable where the person injured will lose income as a result of the accident. Again check to see if the church policy makes such provision. But do check, and do not just take it for granted.

We come next to the most common form of insurance – insurance against damage to, or the destruction of, property. If the club owns the building in which it meets then it will be responsible for insuring the building itself. More often, however, it will belong to the parochial church council. Some PCCs are very good at updating their cover each year, but some recent catastrophes have demonstrated that others are certainly not. Destruction of the hall where you meet could mean the end of the club, so it is in your own interests to ensure that the owner of the building has it adequately covered. Even if the premises are only partially damaged, insurance may not cover the total cost of repair if the building as a whole is under-insured. Some PCCs will ask for a donation towards insurance from the various users. This is only fair and gives even more right to check that insurance is at a realistic level.

Whether they own the building or not, most clubs will possess equipment and this too needs protection. Insurance will normally cover loss of, or damage to, articles by a wide range of causes – fire, lightning, explosion, earthquake, bursting pipes, theft, impact by a vehicle or animal, any person taking part in riot, labour disturbance, civil commotion or any person of malicious intent. The list may read like an extract from the prophets of the Old Testament, but don't think it can't happen.

The kind of insurance called *All Risk* will, for an additional premium, provide cover for articles used away from the home base. This is important if you have relatively expensive equipment such as canoes and tents which are frequently taken off the premises. It could also be that your existing insurance does not cover members and workers when they themselves are off the premises, for example on a residential weekend or club holiday. I have in the past experienced great difficulty in getting appropriate insurance for such events through an ordinary broker. It is not the type of risk many insurance firms wish to undertake, at least not without payment of a large premium. Ecclesiastical Insurance Office Ltd (Beaufort House, Brunswick Road, Gloucester GL1 1JZ, tel. Gloucester 35819), and doubtless some other companies as well, have a special reasonably priced scheme. The cost is small enough to be passed on to individual participants without over-inflating the cost of a trip or holiday. Some church insurance will already cover this, so again check first.

It is usually realized that adequate insurance is needed if the club owns a minibus, but perhaps most church clubs use a fleet of cars driven by adult workers or parents to transport members to events away from home. Do ensure that the drivers have adequate cover and that it is not invalidated by the type of use to which the vehicle is being put. If a car is being lent for the occasion and is being driven by someone other than the owner, checking that insurance cover is still valid is especially important. Few people know the exact terms of their insurance without referring to the policy.

For the sake of completion, we deal finally with a type of insurance that will be necessary in only a few clubs – *Employers' Liability Insurance*. This insurance is required by law if you employ and pay staff. It covers you against claims for negligence by people in your employment. The insurance company will provide you with a certificate of insurance which, again by law, you must display on the premises. Most paid staff in voluntary youth clubs are in fact employed by the local education authority and seconded to the club. In these circumstances liaise with the authority to establish what, if any, is your responsibility for Employer's Liability Insurance.

Records
Even more important than the records you play on the turntable are the records you keep of the club's activities and membership.

Two sorts of financial records should be kept. First, a petty cash book. This should record all items of expenditure incurred by the workers and which come within their own agreed expenditure limit. It is intolerable for a worker to have to seek permission of the chairman or treasurer of the management committee every time he wants to spend two or three pounds. The committee should set a realistic limit (and review it periodically) within which the worker has discretion to spend money on necessary items. An accurate record is essential; many unpleasant altercations start because of a small discrepancy in funds either real or imaginary. An ordinary cash note book is sufficient. It is unwise to hold large sums of money in cash. It is also essential to have a good cash box in which to keep it. Wherever possible receipts for purchases (even if only till receipts) should be obtained and kept with the petty cash book.

The second type of financial record is the Income and Expenditure Account. This will be prepared by the treasurer rather than the club workers, and will be presented to the management committee at least annually at the close of the financial year. It will not itemize every item of income and expenditure but will give the total figures under a number of headings, e.g. 'Subscriptions', 'Canteen takings', 'Insurance', Rent of hall', etc. It will also show balances brought forward from the previous year, together with the amount in hand at the bank and in petty cash at the end of the current financial year.

In my experience it is extremely valuable if the treasurer can prepare a statement of accounts for each meeting of the management committee. It has been said elsewhere (see chapter 3) that a committee cannot exercise management properly unless it is given the information it needs on which to base its decisions. Adequate details of the financial position of the club will be important in numerous circumstances, and the average committee member will find it far easier to assimilate the details if they are on paper in front of him rather than read out by the treasurer. Though even that is preferable to the treasurer simply saying that they can afford to spend a certain sum without giving details.

In addition to those dealing with finance, three other types of records are usual. The most important is a register of members. This will have columns for name, address, telephone number (in case of emergencies), birthday/age, and columns for marking each attendance and whether subs have been paid. At the end of an exhausting club evening it is difficult to remember everyone who attended and even more difficult the following week to recall who it was who did not pay. So a well-kept register is valuable. It can also contain a list of young people waiting to join the club when a vacancy occurs. It is usually better to restrict membership to a manageable number (a maximum of 10 per worker or thereabouts) than to have more than you can cater for.

It is also useful to keep brief notes on club members, recording for example their particular interests or any problems they have had at school or home. Some workers have a column for such notes in the register, but as the register is normally seen by members when they pay their subs I think they are better kept apart and in a secure place. A simple card index may well fit the bill. Great outcries have arisen from time to time about 'secret records', and although a few brief notes kept as an aide-mémoire hardly fall into that category, I have always thought it right to destroy a member's notes carefully when he leaves the club.

Lastly it is useful to keep a log book of equipment. This should record items purchased, the date, the cost and where obtained. Say you buy a set of thirty mugs for serving coffee at the club. Two years later some have been broken or perhaps the membership has increased and you need more. I have heard endless discussions as one inadequate memory is pitted against another in a vain attempt to remember where they were bought and for how much. It is a simple matter to refer to the log book and find details of the supplier and his telephone number.

The Canteen
The canteen is an important part of a club's life not least because it gives those who work in it numerous opportunities for one-to-one contact with the members. Some senior workers give it a low priority, and tend to staff it with the newest or least effective workers, but I maintain that this is

one of the most important jobs in the club. Members choosing sweets or drinks make the ideal situation in which to engage them in conversation, to ask, perhaps, about their family or how school is going. It is also a good opportunity to look for tell-tale signs. One club I ran was attended by children from three or four real problem families. I could tell a lot about how things were at home just by the contact with them at the canteen. Only a few pence to spend, or so much money that it looked like a parent salving his conscience, were equally indicative that all might not be well. Clothes that were dirtier than usual and unmended or dark rings under the eyes from lack of sleep were other tell-tale signs. All this is important if one's aim is to meet the needs of the young people, for in situations of stress they need extra care, understanding and attention. There may also be the opportunity to contact the parents through a home visit and extend one's care to them too.

A canteen area is best set up round a sink if there is one, so that mugs and other utensils can be washed up and kettles filled without leaving the serving area. It is also best sited away from boisterous games where flying balls (or even club members!) can demolish everything. The counter could be an unwanted kitchen unit, or tables if it has to be removed at the end of the evening. Ideally the serving areas should be enclosed on all sides so that members are not tempted to get behind the counter and help themselves. Temptation is lessened too if sweets (and cash) are kept well out of reach. Close to the counter is an ideal place for easy chairs, so that members can sit, talk and consume their purchases. The stock needs to be carefully chosen. Young people generally prefer to buy two or three inexpensive sweets rather than spend all their money at once on a delicious but bank-breaking extravagance. Members of junior clubs particularly like the very small novelty sweets which sell at about $\frac{1}{2}$p each. Likewise with drink, a plastic mug (re-usable) of coke served from a two litre bottle is far less expensive than a pre-packed can. As well as price, the variety needs to be right too. If you do not stock what is wanted, the young people will buy elsewhere and bring it to the club with them. A simple market research exercise, asking the young people what they like, lessens the possibility of boxes of unsaleable stock. If the church or club has a cash and carry card then it should be easy to obtain goods at a reasonable price. Alternatively, a local sweet shop may be prepared to purchase in bulk on your behalf or let you have items at below retail price.

Finally, helping behind the counter can be a useful experience for members, particularly those who do not join readily in other activities. The worker has the opportunity to get to know them better, they make use of some basic mathematical skills, and maybe learn something of how aggravating it is to be at the receiving end of a hoard of people clamouring to be served and who lack elementary courtesy!

Rules and Discipline

Every group of people needs a set of rules however basic, written or unwritten, if members are to exist in harmony with one another. This is very true of youth clubs.

An old story tells of a vicar who was taking a walk one Sunday morning. He came across a rowdy group of young people singing songs to the accompaniment of a guitar played by a youth of dubious cleanliness. At the end of the song the vicar pointed his finger accusingly at the youth and said: 'Young man, today is Sunday, do you not know the fourth commandment?'. 'No, never heard of it', came the reply, 'but sing me a couple of bars and I'll try to play it'.

There are lessons to be learnt from that story. First, you have to know rules before you can obey them, even if the law of the land makes no allowance for ignorance. Club members should be made aware of the rules the moment they join. They could be printed on membership cards or posted on the notice board but whatever method is used they must be made known. Second, rules must be reasonable. The youth in the story, had he known the fourth commandment, would doubtless have thought 'Remember the Sabbath Day, to keep it holy' a somewhat unreasonable law. To the vicar it was perfectly sound, but not to the youth. Similarly with club rules; they must make reasonable sense to the young people. I visited a club recently where one rule was 'No swearing'. To the church members running the club that was quite reasonable, but the young people were the sort who swore, like their parents, frequently and without giving it a thought. Subsequently the evening was punctuated with workers repeatedly telling members to stop swearing. The youngsters obviously did not grasp what all the fuss was about, and most important of all the unreasonableness of the rule lessened the effectiveness of the other more essential ones.

Thirdly, rules must be fairly administered. In the story it is doubtful if pointing an accusing finger and asking about the fourth commandment was the best way of imparting to the youth the importance of respecting Sunday. (It is, to my mind, possible that playing and singing, is *not* in fact breaking the commandment anyway, but that is beside the point.) So in a club situation, rules must be enforced with justice. Rules should be applied to everyone for exceptions undermine the effectiveness of all the rules. And they should apply to workers as well as members. If, for example, no smoking is allowed in the club then workers should abide by the rule too. One set of rules for members and another for workers is intolerable.

Punishments should be fair as well. To be realistic, the range of possible punishments is small. On most occasions a verbal rebuke is all that is possible. Persistent offenders could be suspended for the rest of the evening, or for the next one or two weeks, or even excluded from the club altogether. Alternatively you could visit the parents to discuss the problem. But assess the consequences first. You may never see a suspended member again; that means you have removed any possibility of working with him, and that may not be what you in fact want to achieve. Likewise a

'disciplinary' visit to parents may so change your relationship with the young person that you can no longer get close
enough to him to help him in any way. Above all, threats
should not be made which you have no intention of fulfilling.

At all times it must be remembered that the club is a place
young people come to primarily to enjoy themselves.
Discipline is necessary first to comply with the law – for
example to prohibit the smoking of drugs where this is a
problem, and second to enable the whole group to exist in
harmony. The best way to maintain a well disciplined yet
enjoyable club is not by heavy handed law enforcement, but
by providing the right kind of activities. If a club is enjoyable,
entertaining and educative, then discipline will be less of a
problem.

A Typical Evening

By looking at the outline of a typical club evening we are not
trying to give a blueprint that must be adhered to at all cost.
Individual situations will vary greatly.

For the workers the evening will begin about half an hour
before the members arrive. During this time the club will be
prepared, equipment put out and, if not done previously, jobs
allocated to staff. By the time members arrive everything
should be ready. If the young people have to amuse
themselves for ten minutes because the workers are still
putting out table tennis tables or stocking the canteen, then
they will get restless and discipline throughout the evening
may be difficult as a result.

Subs should be collected and the register marked as they
enter. Doing it later almost inevitably means that someone
slips through the net.

The nature of the programme will vary. Most clubs have a
regular selection of activities such as football, basketball,
table tennis, craft work and the canteen, and add one or two
variable activities which change from week to week. A list of
possible activities is given at the end of this chapter. Much, of
course, depends on what the members themselves want, but I

would suggest that the club that never varies its programme in any respect is not doing all it can to foster the education and growth of its members. Where numbers permit, one or two workers should be free from organization or helping with specific activities so they can just be around to talk with the young people.

Some church open clubs still end with a religious epilogue. 'We have ourselves witnessed such club assemblies, when the atmosphere was favourable, the oratorical skill of the youth worker considerable and the emotional and spiritual mood transcendental. A youth worker may plan carefully for such an occasion, but equally may evoke a spontaneous reaction by calling together the entire club membership in response to some tragic or joyous event in the life of the club community, or some national or world event. Many youth clubs met solemnly together on the evening when President Kennedy was assassinated, and when Manchester United football team died in an air disaster, and joined in prayer without the usual shuffling, simulated coughing or heckling.'[2] Workers need to assess their particular club membership and their own skills before deciding to have epilogues, and should not feel guilty if it seems best to omit them altogether. The very fact of running a club, the way in which it is organized and the personal attitudes of the workers are the most meaningful vehicles for proclaiming one's Christianity; an epilogue may add nothing. Epilogues are positively harmful if members are compelled to attend. I have even visited clubs where workers are posted on the doors to ensure no one leaves before they have imbibed their dose of overt religion. What image of Christianity this might leave in the young person's mind is horrifying to contemplate. Much the same could be said of attendance at church as a prerequisite of club membership.

At the end of the evening the club should finish promptly. After the young people have left and the hall has been tidied, the workers need to spend a few moments together reviewing the evening and planning for next week. The review should include an analysis of which activities were successful and which should not be repeated again, an exchange of views about the young people themselves, which for example need special attention next time, and any other comments about the night's club. It is particularly important that staff have the opportunity to express and share anxieties or problems rather than take them home and dwell on them. Planning for next time will include checking that sufficient staff will be present, what the variable activities will be, who will staff them and what equipment will be needed. Finally the takings will be counted and a record made.

A Selection of Club Activities
In 1942 a book was published entitled *Christian Youth Leadership*.[3] The possible youth club activities it mentioned included filling sandbags, collection and distribution of vegetables for minesweepers, padding crutches and making rugs for searchlight companies. Doubtless the list below will one day be equally out of date because interests change, new activities come into vogue and circumstances alter. In no sense is it a definitive list. It is merely an aid to providing varied activities: one of the secrets of good youth work is a constant employment of imagination which produces new ideas to be used alongside the popular traditional ones.

Games
Most of these can be played indoors or out. Foam balls, obtainable at sports shops, instead of the usual harder ones can be used indoors without detracting too drastically from the vitality of games but with less risk of damage to windows, lights, etc.

Football	Cricket	Baseball
Basketball	Tennis	Hockey
Volleyball	Badminton	Rounders

Rules can be found in any number of books, including some encyclopaedias.

Static Attractions

For want of a better term I have used Static Attractions to describe those various activities that are the general stand-bys in many clubs:

Table tennis

Snooker/Billiards/Pool

Darts

Board and Card Games

Books, comics and magazines (placed on a table in quiet corner for any who wish to sit and read)

Space Invaders and similar electronic games (views vary about whether these should be introduced to clubs). Machines that work only when money is inserted will not pay for themselves unless used more than one night a week. Some clubs, open four or five nights a week, make most of their income from them, as long as the machines are frequently changed so that members do not learn how to win all the time. It is better to rent rather than buy.

Record Player or tape deck (either the club or the members supply the records). Some control is needed over what music is played. A member may leave if his type of music is not heard sometimes during the evening.

Arts and Crafts

Drawing

Painting

Candle making

Cold enamelling

Tie and dye

Plaster-of-Paris moulds

Sewing, dress-making, etc.

Jewellery

Cooking

Soap making

Glass or Metal engraving

Pottery

Carving (be sure of your membership before issuing sharp tools)

Collage making

Printing (various kinds – letterpress, silk screen, lino or wood block, litho)

Carpentry

Picture framing (members bring a picture of their own to frame)

All these can be made available to both sexes. Some activities will be impossible because expensive equipment is needed; you may however find a source from which you can borrow or hire, or it might be possible to take a group to use someone else's equipment. It is important that at least one member of staff is sufficiently knowledgeable in the subject to supervise the activity. Alternatively, there may be a member of the congregation with special skills who would be prepared to help with an activity for, say, four weeks, with the possibility of another set of sessions sometime later, if it proved popular. Some local education authorities have specialist instructors who can be seconded to a club.

In most areas of the country there is a craft shop which will supply material and instruction books.

Special Activities

This list suggests a few club activities of a more unusual nature which do not come into any of the above categories. Some are more appropriately done outside normal club hours, and not necessarily by all the club membership at once. Some can only be done in special locations, perhaps during a club holiday or a day's outing.

Photography – possible activities range from using an instant camera to take pictures of club members and producing a display of them, through a photographic survey of the locality, to sessions learning how to develop and print pictures.

Area Survey – possibly using photography as above, but also including drawing maps, interviewing residents on tape, collecting old pictures, etc.

Community Aid – helping with holiday projects for young children, visiting the housebound, doing shopping for the elderly, etc.

Gardening – either doing gardening for the elderly or handicapped (do ensure adequate supervision), or letting members use a piece of unwanted land to learn about cultivation.

Visits – to places of interest such as a recording studio, a factory (preferably one giving free samples!), an army open day, wild life park, newspaper office, concert, etc.

Video – an occasional evening watching a good film on video can make a welcome change. Do ensure the television is sufficiently large for everyone to see, or connect up more than one set via a junction box. Films can either stand alone or be the basis for discussion. A more creative use of video is possible if you have, or can borrow or hire, a video camera and lights. A small group of members could then make a film of their own – about the club, the area, key figures in the community, a local housing problem, local employers and employment prospects for school leavers, etc.

Computers – an increasing number of young people are skilled in using computers. Use computers for programmed learning, for games, or to help increase members' ability to use and programme them themselves.

Music – encourage appreciation by visits to pop and classical concerts and provide opportunities for members to compose, play or sing. With borrowed or rented equipment it is possible to make high quality recordings of the young people's performances.

Dancing – disco dancing is especially popular, but some members may be interested in other forms such as English folk dancing, classical, national or historical. Again there is scope for either passive appreciation or active participation.

Keep fit – if a suitable instructor is available locally this can be a very attractive activity.

Thematic events – an evening, a day or weekend on a particular theme can be profitable. Outside 'specialists' can be used. The theme could be, say, Indian Culture, and include appropriate music, food, film, posters and entertainment.

Girls' Topics – activities might include make-up, fashion design and modelling, and discussion on pregnancy and abortion.

Sporting activities – a wide range of possibilities exist for special sporting activities which can supplement the normal club programme. These include:

tug-of-war	fencing	archery
cycling	shooting	judo
mountaineering	pony trekking	angling
swimming	sailing	gymnastics
canoeing	gliding	skating

If demand is sufficient and the right resources are available locally it might be possible to incorporate one or more of the above into the regular programme, otherwise they could be offered as 'occasional extras'.

Chapter 5

Worship and Young People

Worship is a word used in a variety of ways, to mean a variety of things. It can be shorthand for 'acts of worship' and in this sense may encompass anything from a formal celebration of Communion in a Cathedral to an informal service of songs, silence and readings in someone's sitting room. Alternatively worship can be used to describe personal acts of devotion; the quiet times the individual has daily with God. Again, it can describe the experience one has when confronted with the grandeur and beauty of nature. Great writers on worship tend to give it a definition, something like 'the response of man to the Eternal' (Evelyn Underhill). It is this kind of definition which underlies all that is said in this chapter. Worship is seen as an experience which makes the human being more aware of God and elicits a response from the worshipper.

One of the chief aims of workers with Christian young people is to develop their understanding and practice of worship, yet young people and worship is a subject which has been given very little attention by writers on liturgy. Few of them allocate more than an occasional comment to children, and most do not mention young people at all.

Recent developments

A long tradition exists of separating younger members from the rest of the Christian family. Since the beginning of the Sunday School movement until the late 1950s children and younger young people were isolated from the worshipping family of the Church. They attended their own instruction classes, normally at a different time from the main service and in a different place. The emphasis was on teaching the basic facts of Christian belief, and little attention was paid to worship save for a token gesture of hymn singing and a corporate prayer or two. Once a month perhaps, or on special occasions such as Easter, Harvest and Mothering Sunday, they attended church for a service to which their parents were invited. This at least went some way towards familiarizing them with the church building but did not bring them into contact with the main worshipping family of the Church. Only on Parade Sundays did those children and young people who were also members of a uniformed organization join in the worship of the adult congregation. On such occasions, though, worship would have additional 'military' overtones, with the presentation of flags, the wearing of uniforms, and non-liturgical processions.

Choirboys and girls, and younger servers, were the exception to the above pattern. Usually they attended every sung service, and entered adult membership of the church with considerable familiarity with its worship. It is perhaps significant that a large number of clergy were formerly choirboys or servers. But conversely it cannot be denied that such regular and repeated contact with church worship from an early age has inoculated some against 'catching' Christianity in later life.

From about thirteen years of age the pattern of provision changed. The choirboy whose voice had broken, or the boy too old for Sunday School, might have found a place as an alto, tenor or bass in the choir; alternatively he could have been a server. Failing that there was probably little opportunity for active participation in worship save sitting in a pew alongside his family or with a gaggle of friends in seats somewhere near the back of the nave or tucked unobtrusively in a side aisle. Girls fared even worse. In many churches there was no place for them in the choir at any age, nor were they acceptable as servers. After Sunday School age their participation in the life of the Church was limited to 'domestic' chores, such as making sandwiches for the summer fair, cleaning the sanctuary carpet or knitting for a sale of work. Or they continued in the Sunday School in some kind of teaching role. Opportunity for active involvement in worship was probably nil.

Many churches offered a fringe benefit to the young in the form of a club night. But without denying that this was useful in itself, like many fringe benefits, it was nothing to do with the central purpose of the organization. Just as provision of a good social club may make employees of an engineering company stay with the firm, but does not directly influence the quality of their factory work and may even highlight the boredom of it, so a club on Friday night did nothing to help the young people to participate in worship, understand it more fully, or grow into worshipping adults.

In some parishes the above situation still prevails in total or in part. Change has resulted, however, from the widespread introduction of the Family Communion as the main Sunday service, a service which by its nature involves, at least theoretically, church members of all ages. Commonly the children are absent for part of the time so they can attend a 'Ministry of the Word' appropriate to their own age. Occasionally their absence extends into part of the Ministry of the Sacrament as well. Whatever the exact local custom, few churches that adopt that kind of pattern make provision for those above fourteen years of age, at least on a regular basis. Again it is their lot to make what they can of local acts of worship alongside fellow worshippers whose ages span in excess of six decades.

Perhaps as an acknowledgement of the fact that the worshipping needs of some young people are not being met by Family Communion, separate young people's worship is organized from time to time. Often such worship is thematic, involves greater 'audience participation', sits lightly to traditional structures, words and music, and is held on a Sunday evening. The hey-day of these services was in the late 1960s, but with fewer young people generally attending church, both the need and the number of potential participants have waned. Even at the height of their popularity, though valuable in themselves, the services did little to help integrate the young into the main-stream worshipping community. The same can be said of Bible classes and similar opportunities for learning.

Worship not Teaching
A principal fault with many Sunday Schools was that they taught children facts but did not develop an ability to worship. Nevertheless their methods of instruction were better than those used with adults, because discussion, questioning and activity were encouraged. It seems that from the earliest times teaching and worship have been inextricably linked. But there is sometimes a tendency to equate the two, so the satisfactory act of worship becomes the one where something new was learnt about the Bible, about a famous Christian believer, or about God's will for humanity. Inevitably the worshipper does learn during the course of worship, but worship – responding to God – is an end in itself and not just a vehicle for teaching and for gaining additional intellectual knowledge.

Young members of the Christian community are built up both by teaching and by worship, and their need to participate in worship is just as great as their need to know facts, perhaps greater. Facts are to do with intellect, even if gained through experience. Worship transcends mental ability or disability, maturity or naïvety. The most obvious short-coming in reformation churches is the over-emphasis on intellectual knowledge. It is only with this firmly in mind that current concerns about young people and worship can be properly considered.

Young People and Adult Worship

A question that most parishes consider from time to time is whether young people should be involved with the worship of the whole Christian community or whether they should worship independently. And, if the answer is that they should join with members of other ages, then to what extent should the form and content of worship be adapted to become attractive to the younger ones.

It first needs to be said that some young people enjoy and find spiritual satisfaction in the standard adult worship of their church. They relate to music which is traditional both in its composition and performance, they have their awareness of God evoked by formal lessons and preaching, and they have perhaps found a niche in which they can actively participate. It could be that their worship would take on another dimension or even greater profundity if they were exposed to other possibilities, but it would be wrong not to respect their position.

Next it is important to ask some searching questions about the quality of the existing adult worship which one is considering encouraging young people to join. Just as the words and deeds of individual adult members of the Christian community will be witnesses to the nature of their faith, so too will their worship speak volumes to the young. Does their worship raise profound questions, provide glimpses beyond distant horizons, enable the power of God to touch the lives of men and women? Does it encourage a response in the day to day life of the worshipper of such depth that their lives are transformed? Does it bind participants together in a true Christian fellowship that transcends simple friendship? Is it obvious that worship really matters to the clergy and congregation? Or does it seem that attendance at worship is to do with unthinking habit, being acceptable to one's friends, or is an 'entry fee' that enables one to be part of local social club? Are the various contributions to worship – the playing of the organ, the singing of the choir, the readings, the sermon, the intercessions – are they done to the utmost of the ability of those concerned, and with due and careful preparation? All too often young people shy away from adult acts of worship in their church because they are of poor quality rather than because of their intrinsic nature.

It is commonly suggested that it would be better for young people to attend separate acts of worship because some parts of adult worship might be beyond their understanding. This concern needs to be balanced with what was said above about teaching and worship. Only if worship is seen incorrectly, as primarily a vehicle for teaching, does the need for intelligible worship seem so great. If worship is 'the response of man to the Eternal' then it can be evoked as well by unintelligible as by intelligible events. However, as was also said above, worshippers do happen to learn during worship and so this too must be borne in mind. Certainly acts of worship should never be made obscure intentionally, and an important lesson can be learnt from the fact that when the content of worship has been adapted to suit young attenders, it tends also to be the time when adults seem especially appreciative. Perhaps those who plan worship over-estimate some of their adults and by so doing, add unnecessary obscurity to worship. Having said that, it is important to remember that a child grows by constantly coming into contact with that which is beyond his understanding. The same can be true of young people and worship.

Separate worship for young people (like worship in a house group, a visit to sung evensong in a cathedral, or joining with worship of another denomination) can expand one's awareness of God and evoke new levels of response. But this must be weighed against the fact that eucharistic worship in particular is first and foremost something done when the whole Christian community comes together.

Participation and Observation

When thinking of young people in the context of Sunday eucharistic worship or in the context of any other type of worship, a frequent concern is that they should be able to participate as fully as possible.

It is easily taken for granted that young people are only satisfied if they can actively take part. As with adults, some are extremely nervous and embarrassed about adopting a leading role, and like all but the most experienced adults, need adequate preparation and practice.

Nor should it be forgotten that what might appear as passive observation of an act of worship can in fact be true participation. The classic example of this is traditional cathedral choral evensong. Virtually every word is said or sung by clergy and choir: the congregation takes little or no active part. But members of the congregation can be said to worship because they participate with heart and mind. It cannot be denied that for some, such services are the most helpful aid to worship. It is not necessary to be singing, reading or leading the prayers in order to worship.

The tendency in some churches to make young people into liturgical sea lions who perform for the adults – giving the adults a warm sense of satisfaction that theirs is a lively church which encourages participation by the young – should be resisted at all costs. A good rule for all-age worship is that young people should participate no more *and no less* than other worshippers.

Liturgy and Society

Society tends to want its religious institutions and their rites to uphold the *status quo*. In some quarters this is exactly the role adopted by acts of worship. Serious questions can and should be asked about whether this is not contrary to the very nature of Christianity. The Christian is called to be in the world but not of it, and corporate and private worship should be part of the process by which the world is held up for critical analysis in the light of Christian truths and prophetic insights. Christian worship is the act of a community committed to transforming the nature of the world and its inhabitants.

One of the commonest characteristics of young people today is their dissatisfaction with the world as it is. They ask searching questions about topics such as the distribution of wealth, lack of employment, the threat of nuclear war and the diminishing freedom of the individual. Certainly not all are motivated by a Christian desire for truth and justice, but nevertheless only acts of worship which reflect their own questioning are likely to sound sympathetic notes within them.

Variation and Excitement

The worship of the Taizé Community in France, which has been so popular with young people in the last decade or so, claims to be provisional. It is always subject to review and revision. This makes for a flexible approach to worship which is not always possible when one is confined to the forms prescribed in a book which has undergone a lengthy history of approval by committee and synod. The Church of England seems likely to be a 'community of the books' (Prayer Book and Alternative Service Book) for the foreseeable future. So while recognizing the need for other forms which will add changing variety to the worship of all ages, it is also necessary for the young to develop a familiarity (through experience) with official services. Those who are fed only a diet of home-spun acts of worship will find the transition to adult worship a difficult one.

But whether worship is in a form prescribed or is the creation of those participating, the place of excitement and variation needs constant consideration. An unaccompanied Good Friday service in a church stripped of its ornaments, followed by the colour, light and music of Easter morning worship is one traditional recognition of this need. Experience shows how well young people respond to the unusual in worship. The experience of a dawn Eucharist at the end of an all-night vigil is powerful and evocative, as too can be an open-air service, a late-night service by candlelight, or a carol service in a children's hospital. These are but a few examples of ways new life can be injected into the routine of worship thereby evoking greater awareness of God and eliciting a deeper response.

A young person who has only experienced worship in his own parish church has yet to savour all the possibilities. Part of his Christian education should be to taste the worship of the village community, the modern estate, the house group, the cathedral, the formal and the informal, the Methodist, the Roman, the Baptist, the Quaker and the Orthodox.

Sensitivity and Embarrassment

Adolescence is a time of heightened sensitivity and a brash external appearance is most frequently a mask rather than a true reflection of inner confidence. All workers with the young ignore this fact at their peril, not least those who have responsibility for involving young people with public acts of worship.

It is easy to underestimate, or even to be unaware of, the embarrassment that can be caused by customs or actions which long-established church-goers take for granted. Some young people are intensely embarrassed by appearing in public, even within the confines of the church building, dressed in cassock and surplice or a white alb. It sets them apart at a time in their development when it is important to be acceptable to their peers. And boys, conscious of a need to express their masculinity, can suffer traumatically from being seen in long flowing robes which have definite feminine overtones. Embarrassment is less when the young person has had sufficient experience of church dress so that robes have distinct ecclesiastical associations which surmount all others, but one needs to be very aware of such things when dealing with a newcomer.

Again, as has been mentioned before, reading a lesson,

leading the intercessions, or any other activity which exposes the individual to the worshipping public, can be far more traumatic than any experienced person can recall. Nor is taking part in an informal group always an easier experience. The number of people watching and listening may be fewer but small groups lack the impersonal quality of the large gathering. Sufficient preparation and rehearsal followed by reassuring praise will help to build confidence.

Another source of embarrassment is the process of going forward to receive Communion and the walk back to one's seat in full view of the congregation. Probably only familiarity will lessen the feeling, so experience of it as a young child is beneficial. Young people who are new to the worshipping community, and are as yet un-confirmed, may find it particularly embarrassing to come forward to receive a blessing – usually given to children – when their contemporaries are handed the elements. If sidesmen and others are sufficiently sensitive they will not put undue pressure on the young person who prefers to stay in his seat.

A fourth common cause for embarrassment for both adults and young people alike is uncertainty about the order of service. Standing or kneeling in the wrong places, or flicking through the pages of the service book in an attempt to find the next prayer, can give rise to awkwardness. A well-presented service sheet or the announcement of rubrics and page numbers can help alleviate this (although endless interpolations can be exceedingly wearisome).

None of these causes of embarrassment should be underestimated.

The Setting for Worship

The builders of great cathedrals knew how worship can be hindered by unconducive surroundings and encouraged by uplifting ones. Attention needs to be given to comfort, both in seating and heating, not because either generally evokes worship, but because uncomfortable seating and poor heating can easily inhibit it. In addition there is little doubt that some young people have been put off church attendance by the physical discomfort incurred when making an occasional visit for a baptism or wedding. The younger generation, used to central heating at home and more creature comforts than their parents and grandparents enjoyed, are affected by such things more than in the past. Some people would argue that to 'soften' the environment of worship is rather spineless, but in reality one stands more chance of encouraging young people to attend church by adapting to their expectations than by hoping to persuade them that a cold shower regime is good for them.

Inevitably in ancient buildings it may not be possible to adapt the environment to suit modern tastes, but then there is the compensation of being in a place that has been hallowed by countless ages of worship. But whatever the building – church, hall, or private dwelling – many are the ways in which the setting can be exploited to encourage worship. Lighting is important and experiments can be made using localized light or candles, or almost total darkness. One incumbent, newly inducted, found a flourishing drama club on Saturday nights but virtually nobody at Communion on Sunday mornings. He persuaded the club's electricians to install stage lighting in church and to create variations in intensity and colour as the service progressed. He soon had a full church on Sundays. An extreme example perhaps, but that true story illustrates the often-forgotten importance of lighting, not as a gimmick but as one means of evoking worship in man's often reluctant heart.

The Church has for centuries acknowledged the importance of colour in worship by choosing symbolic shades for different times of its year. Movement too has a time-hallowed place in worship, in the gospel procession, the move towards the altar to receive the sacrament, facing east for the creed, bowing the head at the name of Jesus, the genuflect, the signing with the cross and the raised hand of blessing or absolution, to say nothing of liturgical dance and drama. As aids to worship, colour and movement in all their potential uses and forms should be considered seriously not least when dealing with young people.

Two features of God – his closeness and his 'otherness' – have received varying degrees of emphasis by different branches of the Church at different times. The most recent trend in the Church of England has been towards God the One who draws near. Every young person should, through worship, have the chance to respond to both aspects of God's nature, and the setting of worship may have much to do with which facet of God is emphasized. A grand parish church speaks of a great and distant being while a group met together in someone's sitting room may be more aware of 'God with us'. Variety in venues as well as in styles of worship will help to present a full picture of God to young and old alike.

Music

Services specifically for young people or with particular concern for the young are frequently associated in people's minds with 'pop' church music, and its presence or absence can easily become an area of conflict within a congregation.

To some adults modern church music still means those hymns and tunes written in the late 1950s and early 1960s by the Twentieth Century Church Light Music Group such as *Living Lord*, and the music for *O Jesus I have promised* and *At the Name of Jesus*. The best of these have now found a place in new collections of hymns for all ages while the majority, described by the composers as 'transient music', though very successful when first performed, are neither modern any longer, nor musically superior to their alternative older tunes. Their place has been taken to some extent by simpler songs originating in the Taizé Community and elsewhere. They are mainly in the folk idiom and have little or no relationship with modern commercial pop music which embraces a range of styles which it would be difficult to incorporate into worship.

The criterion to be applied to any music being considered for use in worship is 'can it help to increase one's awareness of God and to elicit a response from the worshipper?' Music, with or without words, that fails to meet this test can have only an incidental place in Christian worship, and at worst can be no more than a gimmick.

It must be remembered that some young people prefer, and find more helpful, liturgical music in the classical idiom rather than in a pop style. Likewise much modern church music, in either the folk or classical tradition, appeals across a wide age range. The carols of John Rutter are a good example of this; undoubtedly modern, with a wide appeal, and inducive of worship. Modern music need not divide young from old. As with traditional forms of worship, so with well-established styles of liturgical music, young people do well to have experience of these, as well as being encouraged to experiment with new alternatives; only then will transition to membership of the adult worshipping community be relatively easy. Whether one is thinking of dearly-loved hymns of the last century, organ voluntaries, anthems or even the chanting of the psalms, young people are most likely to find them helpful if their performance is good.

A final note is necessary about the use of instruments other than the organ to accompany congregational singing. A youth service or those parts of an ordinary service where young people have a specific musical contribution to make, are often an excuse for making the organist redundant and replacing him with pianist, guitarist, or other instrumentalist. Certainly some modern church music is better suited to a more flowing and lyrical accompaniment than an organ can provide, and little is to be gained aesthetically by making the organ sound like something from a mid-twentieth century Odeon. Nevertheless few solo instruments provide the volume of sound that can lead a congregation effectively in even a moderate size church. Either groups of instruments should be used or a choir be rehearsed to give the sort of lead most congregations find essential. The usual alternative is shy and half-hearted participation which adds nothing to worship.

Worship for Young People alone

The need for young people to be familiar with traditional forms of worship and music has already been stressed. Acts of worship for the young alone must have benefits for those taking part which cannot be had elsewhere, or there is little point in having them. One of the chief benefits of such occasions is that they can give young people the opportunity to devise the form and content of worship themselves. Generally this is far more beneficial than adults preparing a talk, choosing hymns and readings and determining the structure in a way they *think* will be helpful to the young people.

One formula I have used myself is as follows. Around 2 p.m. on a particular Sunday afternoon I meet with all the young people who want to volunteer to construct an act of worship (this may not include everyone who eventually comes to the service). Alternatively, the planning meeting could be held the Sunday before or one evening during the preceding week. The time allotted to planning is deliberately short because that creates pressure which in turn makes for more intensive and fruitful thinking and ensures that interest does not wane. The young people are divided into groups of three or four and are given about ten minutes to agree on a theme for worship. At the end of the time the small groups come back together again and the various ideas are written up on a flip chart. It is then necessary to arrive at the one generally acceptable theme. Some may be identical or so similar as to be easily combined. Some groups may prefer another group's theme to their own, or it may be necessary to vote. Unsuccessful ideas can be kept in mind for future occasions.

The second stage is to develop the theme. Again divide the young people into groups (not necessarily the same as before). At least one group will be necessary to deal with each aspect of worship – the singing, the readings (sacred and secular), the prayers, and also perhaps drama and dance, etc. Each group is asked to write or choose material on the pre-determined theme for their particular part of worship. If, for example, the theme is 'peace' one group will search for hymns or songs, the second for suitable biblical passages, the third for appropriate secular readings, the fourth will find or write prayers, and so on. It is surprising the amount of material most young people can recall from memory or create from their imaginations without external aid, but I always have a selection of books, music and a concordance to hand to give assistance when necessary. (School assembly anthologies are very useful.) Occasionally someone has to make a flying visit home to get material they particularly want, or alternatively when the planning session takes place well in advance of the service it can be obtained during the intervening period.

The third stage is to put all the individual contributions into some kind of order and to decide who will do what. Usually some 'editing' is required to make the act of worship a manageable length. Lastly the contributions are rehearsed (rehearsals can take place at another time if the service does not follow later the same day).

When the planning and the service take place on the same afternoon and evening it is useful to break for refreshments mid-way. At the appointed time, say 6.30 p.m., the act of worship begins. It could be that only those involved with planning will attend, it could attract other young people as well, and older members of the church might also value an invitation to attend. In my experience a 'link-man' is required to hold the different elements together and this could well be the person – adult or young person – who organized the planning session. His role is to state the theme, to announce hymns and to introduce other items with words such as: 'the theme of peace is taken up in the second reading from John's Gospel chapter 14', or 'Martin is going to read a poem he has written called *There is no peace*'. Groups vary, and inevitably some will need more adult assistance to produce an act of worship than will others.

The mode of presentation is almost as important as choice of material. So at the planning stage the whole group should have discussion about musical instruments to be used, the use of lighting, seating arrangements, and visual presentations of the theme – posters, slides, etc. If time permits a small group might undertake designing and producing a service leaflet.

Experience suggests this is one of the most successful ways of helping young people to worship corporately.

Private Worship
Much of this chapter has been about corporate worship, but it is important that private worship is not forgotten. There is a need to encourage in each young person a pattern of regular private devotion. Probably no better guiding formula exists than the well-established 'ACTS'. 'A' stands for Adoration – an essential element in 'the response of man to the Eternal'. 'C' is Confession – the acknowledgement that the worshipper has fallen short of the glory of God. 'T' represents Thanksgiving – the important directing of one's thoughts to the benefits one has received, and 'S' is for Supplication – asking of God those things needed by mankind. A formula such as this lessens the tendency, often created by childhood bedtime prayers, to turn private devotion into an endless series of requests for self, family and friends.

Within this framework a variety of aids can be used to facilitate worship: Bible study, secular readings, meditation on a written passage or an object, silence, the keeping of a list or notebook of subjects for intercessions, books of formal prayers, recorded music, and bringing before God the needs of the world with the aid of an open newspaper. As with public worship, variation and excitement can evoke devotion. Rising early before the world is awake, meditating in the darkness of night or in the open air on a summer morning can all prevent spiritual staleness. Yet a daily discipline of private worship is something most young people find difficult.

For the Christian every part of life contains an element of worship; it is not something restricted to an hour on Sunday or a few minutes each day. Conversely, though man can be aware of God and respond to him at any time and in any place, neither the hour on Sunday nor the private times during the week are thereby rendered unnecessary.[1]

Chapter 6

Confirmation and Spiritual Growth

Nurturing the young in the faith, whether as a preliminary to Confirmation or not, is one of the greatest tasks of the Church. Individual churches cannot claim success unless their young people are being helped to grow into 'well rounded' human beings with knowledge and experience of Christianity.

Confirmation at what age?
In the Church of England as a whole the age for Confirmation varies enormously. Eleven is usually the youngest age (though exceptions are made) but, leaving aside the encouraging number confirmed as adults, most seem to be in the thirteen to fifteen age range. Frequently heard comments about Confirmation being nothing more than a 'passing-out ceremony' suggest that this is not the best age (and that preparation and follow-up are not as good as they might be). Certainly educationally and psychologically it is the worst possible time.

Confirmation is about the re-affirmation of promises taken on one's behalf when an infant; it is about proclaiming publicly one's beliefs and loyalty; it is about declaring one's intention to devote one's life to creating God's kingdom on earth. The average thirteen to fifteen-year-old has neither the simple unquestioning faith of the pre-adolescent nor the mature faith of an adult. As we have seen elsewhere in this handbook, adolescence is a time of change, a time when new ideas are tried out, a time for discovering oneself. Making a public commitment to anything sits uneasily alongside these marks of adolescence. It is hardly surprising that some drift away.

As a result of this problem a number of suggestions have been made (e.g. in the Ely Report) about admitting children to Communion before they are confirmed. This practice also enables children (especially those of Christian parents) to take part fully in the Sunday worship of the whole Christian community. One of the disadvantages of the increased popularity of Family Communion is that not all the family are in fact treated the same – it creates first-class members of the family and second-class ones. Most parishes which have experimented with early admission to Communion at seven or eight years old (where permitted to do so by the Bishop) have found that the fall-off in early and mid-teens happens less. But this may be because early admission tends to be accompanied by an on-going course of instruction from shortly before first Communion onwards.

It is difficult to know what is the ideal age for Confirmation. Around eighteen would probably be the earliest time – the age when young adults are considered capable of voting and making other adult decisions. Some would argue for a few years later when a person has more experience of the world of work. But when all is said and done, mature commitment is the main factor not physical age. Nevertheless the pattern of Confirmation in early teens is well established. So although psychologically and educationally the present pattern is unsatisfactory, I suspect the Church of England will only move away from it very slowly. In recognition of this, what follows here bears in mind that young Confirmation candidates might be anything from eleven to about twenty years old. We must make what we can of the existing practices.

How long should preparation last?

Course material currently available is designed for anything from ten weeks to about two years. Not even the longest of these is sufficient in itself. In a parish there should be an on-going series of study groups for young people (indeed for all ages). Every young person should be encouraged to take part in a group appropriate to his or her age and ability, whether or not they are consciously aiming at Confirmation. This is the least a parish can offer to its young people if they are to grow into well-informed, thinking and committed members. This approach also lessens the pressure on them to be confirmed whether it is appropriate or not. In many churches as soon as someone reaches a pre-determined age – eleven, thirteen or whatever – the three-line Confirmation whip goes out. Pressure from their peers and the vicar (often very subtle pressure) ensures they become Confirmation statistics. If there are continuing study groups, Confirmation becomes a milestone along the way (reached at different times according to the speed travelled) rather than the final destination.

The role of the Church Community

Just as important as the quality of study groups is the quality of the local Christian community. If it is full of vitality, welcoming and caring, then a young person is likely to be attracted to it and remain loyal to it and all it stands for. This cannot be said too often. Educationalists emphasize the amount we learn, almost unconsciously, from the world around us. So, young people learn from their experiences of the Christian community: from these they will discover what it means to be a Christian. If local members paint a dismal picture, the young will develop a taste for neither the painting nor the artist.

One way the importance of the Christian community will be reflected is through their involvement in study groups for the young. A long tradition associates Confirmation classes and the like with the vicar or curate. The parish priest has an important part to play in helping the young to learn, but usually much is to be gained by the involvement of laity as well. If there are on-going study groups for different ages then no one person – not even parson – could adequately lead them all. Some parishes have lay men and women well-equipped to help the young learn, others *will* have them as more attention is given to training them for such work, and all parishes have lay people with something – however simple – to share.

There is a case too for older young people being involved with younger groups. They could share their experiences of witnessing at school or work; they could talk about why they decided to be confirmed; they could lead a group on a specific topic after adequate help and preparation. They gain from thinking topics through sufficiently well that they can share them, and the younger members benefit from seeing those only a little older witnessing to their faith.

Church-going parents will value being kept in touch with what study groups are doing, and if Confirmation is being contemplated that is a good time for a home visit by one of the clergy or the group leader. The parish should not expect a young person under eighteen to make a public declaration of belief without prior consultation with parents. This is a God-given opportunity to share with non-Church attenders something of what following Christ means. Parents often welcome guidance on suitable confirmation presents, and if the church is giving a present to each candidate – a good expression of the love of the whole community – then parents could well be told in advance what it will be. Some churches have found it valuable to have an annual reunion party (and/or service) for past Confirmation candidates, and parents could be invited as well.

Content of training
In the past Confirmation training has often over-emphasized the need to learn facts: catechisms with their long lists of items to be learnt have contributed. Thorough and complete nurturing in the faith will include both head and heart knowledge. There will be facts to learn with the mind, *and* experience of living in the Christian way.

Experience of living the Christian life
Living the Christian life is not easy, especially for young people who have no support at home. The church community must introduce young people to those elements of the Christian life which have traditionally upheld and encouraged belief. In Chapter 5 the importance of *worship* has already been stressed. The study group should also be a worshipping group. Sometimes the only nod in this direction comes from an opening and closing prayer, all the rest of the time being given to learning facts. As was said in the previous chapter, young people can experience a whole new dimension to worship when doing it informally with a group of friends.

Experience of *prayer* is important too. Many young people (and I suspect many older ones too) have a very narrow view of prayer. For them it is primarily asking God for things which they haven't the money or the willpower to obtain for themselves. Prayer is of course much broader. It expresses thanks to God, shows adoration, demonstrates contrition, shows our desire for others and ourselves to be blessed, demonstrates our dependence on God. As Neville Ward writes (*The Use of Praying*, Epworth, 1967, p. 13) 'If we pray at all it is because we have been brought into a praying community'. The whole local church must be a praying community; so must the study group. From there the young people will learn by experience what it is to pray.

Regular use of the Bible is a habit (in the best sense of the word) to be encouraged. Working in a study group young people should learn not just the barren facts – the number of books in the Bible, the names of the minor prophets, etc. - but how to use the Bible as part of their private and corporate spiritual life. In their group they will experience the study of particular passages - with one or more of the members perhaps preparing a study for the whole group. And they will explore themes, learning to search around with the use of a concordance (or just their memories) to discover what different Old and New Testament writers have to say on a subject. In addition to group study, they will be encouraged to read the Bible alone. Bible Notes (such as those prepared by the Bible Reading Fellowship) could be given out at group meetings for members to use each day. An occasional discussion on how individuals are progressing, or on particular problems they might encounter with the next week's readings, will help. The aim should be to produce a familiarity and respect for Scripture which befits the people of the Book.

Meditation and the constructive use of *silence* are two more activities which a study group could usefully experience. They might meditate on a word - for example, 'light', 'peace', 'hope', or on a verse of the New Testament. They could meditate while music is played or while watching an object such as a lighted candle, a flower or a photo or painting. As a first introduction to silence and meditation the group leader may lead them, but this can be dispensed with later as group members learn the skills. Again, from experience in the group, young people will learn the techniques for themselves.

An important part of a group's learning will centre on *Christian Action*. Whatever else Christianity is, it is a religion which inspires action. Throughout history its followers have been empowered to give love where love is absent, to care for broken spirits, broken bodies and broken relationships, to struggle for justice and peace, to fight against man's inhumanity to man. Any study group for young people should aim to give its members a glimpse of this aspect of the Christian life. And having glimpsed it, members should be encouraged to play their part. Once again the best way to learn about such things is to experience them.

The group could explore various ways in which the Church is involved in the community. Members could visit a church youth club (especially if not members of one themselves) and talk to the workers about how they see the work as an expression of their Christian Faith. Similarly they could visit a church school to investigate the Church's role in education. They could visit *in situ*, or invite to the group, Christians involved in the police, local or central politics, social and public services, journalism, medical care in hospital, clinic or surgery, etc. On each occasion members could prepare in advance questions they want to ask both about the specific activity and about the way in which it is an expression of Christian love and concern. Further time can be spent with the vicar, curate, deaconess, parish worker and other laity about how they express their beliefs in concrete action in the community.

By far the best way of learning about Christianity in Action is to take part in some activity oneself. Group members should be encouraged to do this. Any number of possibilities exist according to local needs and the age of the young people. They could help with a junior youth club; in pairs visit elderly people – do shopping for them or gardening; fund-raise for a local charity; go carol singing to buy toys for a children's hospital; baby-sit so parents have a break from their children for an evening. Time should be given for the whole group to reflect on experiences and to provide mutual support.

Facts for learning

The second half of a balanced Christian diet is learning some facts about Christian belief. Theology is an exceedingly complex and complicated subject. Group leaders will be conscious of their group's ability and lead them only as far as they can sensibly go. St Paul spoke of giving milk to 'infants in Christ' instead of solid food for which his audience was not ready. We do well to follow his example, but conversely we should not fail to make demands and set high aims. Christians are often put to shame by Jehovah's Witnesses and Mormons who know their doctrine so thoroughly.

Many Confirmation classes (and the courses on which they are based) tend to be over dominated by 'domestic matters' – what the vicar wears, the parts of the church building, what the Communion vessels are called, the services in ASB, etc. There is a place for these things in any study group's course, but we fool ourselves if we think young people find them grippingly interesting. We also run the risk of presenting a very parochial and inward looking picture of Christianity. A varied course will probably include the following: Myself, Fellowship, Jesus, Man and God, Faith, Sacraments, Discipleship (from *Confirmation Cook Book* (see p. 145)).

Additionally those members who have decided to be confirmed will need specific teaching about Confirmation and Communion. They should know about the services – their history, meaning and importance, and receive instruction on the practicalities of taking part in the services (many will of course be familiar with the Communion service already). If the pattern advocated earlier is being followed, i.e. *all* young people are encouraged to be involved with study groups, then it is usually best to set up a short-term group just for Confirmation candidates to supplement the more general groups.

Techniques

It is all very well knowing *what* to impart, but equally important to know *how* to do it. The following is a list of possible methods:

1. *Talks* This traditional method of imparting information is no longer the great favourite of educationalists. Research has shown that people remember only a small proportion of what they hear – far less than things they see, write or experience. But talks may be used sparingly so long as it is

remembered that the attention of young people tends to wane very quickly, and that speakers need to be good. Talks should never be an easy substitute for spending time to create a more effective way of learning.

2. *Discussion* Discussion can be aimless or well-planned; barren or well-informed. A group leader should have a good idea at the beginning of the topics a discussion should cover; he will then be able to move the discussion on according to the time available, and ensure that 'red herrings' do not detract from main issues. Ideally a discussion leader should spend time getting to know the subject beforehand. He should not direct discussion towards the conclusions *he* wants, but should be ready to feed in additional factual information or pertinent questions when required. Some discussions will draw on the experience of group members but others will require all participants to do some 'home-work' in advance. An important role for the leader is to draw out the shy and to restrain the talkative – always he will do this sensitively and never ridicule anything anyone says. It is useful at the end to jot down on a flip chart any conclusions from the discussion. Later these can be typed and distributed to members to keep for reference.

3. *Audio-visual Aids* Every group leader should have access to audio and visual aid catalogues, whether held centrally by the parish or in his own possession. These should include lists of films, filmstrips, slides, tapes, posters and (though not strictly visual-aids) educational games. Most catalogues give a brief synopsis of the material and these will help a leader choose what is most appropriate. Obviously he will also need access to various pieces of equipment – projectors, cassette player, and ideally a flip-chart and an overhead projector. If the parish does not have its own teaching equipment it is often possible to borrow from a nearby school. Access to a photo-copier is also valuable so that good quality handouts can be produced.

Audio-visual aids should never be used as gimmicks – just something to arrest the attention of the group. They should be an integral part of the teaching programme with a specific contribution to make.

It is essential that leaders order material they want well ahead: the most popular material on loan could be booked up just when needed. A leader should allow sufficient time to look at the material thoroughly before using it. It is not unknown to find that a set of slides, for example, which sounded ideal in the catalogue, turns out to be inappropriate or in need of editing. He should also ensure that equipment is in working order, and spend time just before a group arrives checking on blackout, volume levels, visibility of the screen and the position of seats. The interest of a group can be lost during the time it takes to thread a film projector or find the right track on a tape: this should be done in advance.

Leaders should ask themselves if a visual aid will stand alone or whether it needs follow-up, and if so of what type. It could lead into discussion (some material is specifically designed for this), or could be followed by individually completed worksheets, or by silence, meditation or prayer. The aim will be to make the fullest possible use of the audio-visual material. Over-use of such material is a danger. Young people can get bored with a total diet of visual aids just as with anything else.

A note on cost Some visual aids can be had on free loan but others are quite expensive to hire or buy. If a parish runs three or four study groups for different ages their annual outlay on aids could be considerable. An integrated programme can help because, with careful planning, more than one group can use material while it is in the parish. Additionally, a little work to produce a list of resources owned by churches in the deanery or by other denominations, can pay dividends. Ultimately a parish council needs to decide the priority it gives to training, and experience suggests that the money can usually be found if commitment is sufficiently great.

4. *Worksheets* Active participation in the process of learning is more effective than being a passive recipient. Using

worksheets is one way of achieving active participation by group members. Some worksheets are produced commercially either alone or as part of a teaching pack. But it is fairly easy for a leader to prepare worksheets for his group.

The type of questions that can be asked are broadly of two kinds. The first is about personal attitudes. 'What would I do if I go to a telephone box and find $\frac{1}{2}$p, 5p, 20p, £1, £100? Why would I act like that?' The aim here is not to get just one word answers but to help the participants delve into their own personality and philosophy of life. Answers to personal questions can be embarrassing, so it is important with an adolescent group to allow them to keep their answers to themselves. The purpose is to help individuals know themselves better, so there is no necessity to read out responses, but some may be willing to share what they have written in discussion.

The second type of question is of a more factual nature, for example on a film the group has just seen. Again, questions will mainly be of the 'Why?' variety – Why did Sheila leave home? Why did Jesus tell the disciples to let the children stay? Why was Bonhoeffer killed? Questions which begin with 'Who?' or 'What?' tend to result in less useful one word answers. 'Why?' questions encourage thinking. Sometimes a photo or picture can be reproduced and given to group members with questions relating to it.

Worksheets can be designed for use during group meetings or for use by members while away from the group. The latter might include a set of questions for friends at school or work on *their* attitudes (the results could be analysed when the group meets); questions to adult members of the congregation about beliefs, attitudes, experiences; questions which necessitate examining the daily papers or television news for a week. What coverage did the Church get? What *good* news was there? What were the cause of discord and conflict? (The 'Why?' questions would follow when the answers were discussed in the group.)

Worksheets are not school tests. The atmosphere in which

they are done should be different, and except on factual points no impression should be given that there are right and wrong answers. Sometimes it is appropriate for group members to work in pairs or small groups, each person contributing to one set of replies.

A final warning: beware of the illiterate! Worksheets presuppose some writing skill which not all groups, or not all members of a group, will have. For those who can cope with them they are valuable and thought provoking but a sheer embarrassment to those who cannot. An alternative is to have a verbal quiz. Not the sort produced com-mercially – give ten biblical names beginning with Z, but ones which again produce careful and useful thought.

5. *Art Work* Some mention has already been made of using visual art, as an aid to meditation and as a subject for worksheets. There is also the more active use of art as a learning technique. Instead of responding to an existing work, group members create their own. Younger ones might enjoy painting, or colouring a picture on a theme; older ones could construct a collage either individually or as a group activity. Themes could be biblical or historical, could reflect recent experiences, or illustrate a piece of music or a song being played in the background. Creative art work is not a time-filler but a valuable educational aid. It must, however, have a purpose, e.g. to help members express their inner feelings, or to help young people remember an important fact. When pictures are finished (a time limit sometimes helps to fire creativity), that is not necessarily the end of the activity. Perhaps at a later meeting members could talk to the group about their work – what it represents; why they did it in that particular way. When a whole group has jointly produced one picture, a useful discussion could follow on who was most directive, who stayed in the background, and how decisions were made about theme, content, colours, etc. Finally pictures could be displayed in the meeting place or church. They could be used as a visual aid during Sunday worship.

6. *Bible Study* Bible study has already been discussed above as one of the 'techniques' young people themselves need to learn. It is also, of course, a principal method of learning about Christian beliefs. In addition to the Bible a group could study selected passages from elsewhere – the writings of the saints and doctors of the Church, and of modern authors including novelists and poets. This requires a fairly high standard of literacy and will not be suitable for all groups, but a couple of pages from a comic can even be used to spark off discussion on moral issues or on inter-personal relationships.

7. *Learning by Heart* Learning by heart is not the same as learning by rote. Many members of a generation or two ago can still remember lengthy quotations learned at Sunday School and Confirmation class. They may not, however, *understand* what they remember. This was the fault of learning by rote; it made unintelligent memories. But there is value in learning facts by heart if understanding is present too. Many Christians usefully recall quotations from the Bible, Prayer Book, or hymn book in times of crisis, or when talking with others about their faith.

Group members could learn a text each week (preferably one that relates to the present topic under discussion). There is little value, though, in testing how well it has been remembered. Texts are learned to help the individual in his Christian life, not so that he can pass some divine exam. If members see the value of learning by heart, that in itself should provide sufficient motivation. Many people know how much easier it is to remember words sung to music rather than spoken or written. Good use can be made of this fact. Numerous Christian songs in the modern idiom are available, and use of one or two of them during group meetings cannot only aid worship but help to fix basic truths in the memory.

8. *Educational Games* Learning through games is another example of it being better to be an active participant than a passive recipient. These are not ordinary games but ones

specifically designed to aid learning. Some are produced commercially, such as *The Grain Drain* (a joint production by Oxfam, Christian Aid and CAFOD) which stimulates serious thought about the commercial relationship which exists between rich and poor countries. Other games needing few physical resources can be found outlined in various publications (see Appendix 4). Such games are extremely useful and an under-used technique.

9. *Drama and Role Plays* A number of organizations and publishers produce plays and similar material for use in Christian groups – e.g. CMS, Scripture Union and Celebration Publishing (57 Dorchester Road, Lytchett Minster, Poole, Dorset BH16 6JE). As with educational games, the aim is to stimulate thought and aid learning. Usually they are performed for the benefit of the participants, not for an audience.

A less structured use of drama is to ask a group to devise a short, unscripted play of their own on a set theme chosen either by the group leader or by the members. Ten minutes or so of preparation, during which characters are allocated and the basic outline agreed, is followed by 'the performance'. The advantage of this method is that the participants can use 'the play' to express their own views. Suitable themes are love, anger, self-sacrifice, and moral subjects such as stealing, dishonesty and conflict. Usefully the play could be followed by time for reflection on how members portrayed characters, why they interpreted the theme as they did, and alternative ways it might have been developed.

In role plays scenarios are devised, and individuals are given detailed characters to portray. After some moments for preparation, members enact the scene. For example, one person could take the role of a hospital chaplain, and another a woman who has just given birth to her first child. The rest of the group watches as the two enact the chaplain's visit. Or again, one could be an embittered elderly man, two others young people unloved at home and another the local beat policeman. The elderly man has dialled 999 because of the noise outside his bungalow. After a 'play' the whole group can discuss what has been said and done. This method can be used equally well to bring alive biblical stories.

10. *Group Experiences* Members of a group will have experiences from time to time which can be the perfect starting point for group learning. One girl in a group I led started talking about her mother's illness – why did God allow such things? We abandoned the programme for that meeting and talked about what was nearest to her heart – some of the other members knew her mother quite well. It was one of the most valuable sessions that group had. Or again, a member might have a brother or sister about to be married or a niece or nephew soon to be baptized. It might be possible for members to attend the service and then to follow it up with discussion, worksheets, art work or Bible study.

In addition, a group can be given deliberately a corporate experience to help them learn. This could be a visit to a film being screened locally, or to a theatre. It could be a tour of a local hospital, a visit to the country or city, or an all-night hike. As well as being times when valuable informal conversations take place, visits and trips out can easily contribute to the learning programme when developed imaginatively. Of all such activities the residential event away from home gives the widest range of learning experiences (see Chapter 8).

Conclusion

The idea of on-going study groups (in which specific Confirmation training plays only a small part) may seem like a lot of hard work. It is. But the importance of the Christian Faith and the importance of young people argue for supreme effort. They also argue for the training of adults so that they can, with the parish priest, form a team of well-equipped educators constantly striving to build up the local Christian community.

Some rural parishes will have few young people, and

transport problems which prohibit joining with other parishes. On-going study groups as suggested above could then be impossible. An alternative is to join with nearby churches for occasional all-day or weekend sessions. The content and techniques would remain the same.

Chapter 7

New Ventures

From time to time a parish will consider undertaking a new youth work venture – a new club, counselling service, advice centre, a series of residential events, or similar. Or occasionally it may instigate a thorough review of existing work to assess its usefulness. This chapter aims to suggest a simple process of research which will help new or revised projects get off to a good start: it is easily adapted to individual circumstances. Planning properly for a new venture (or undertaking a thorough review) can eliminate much wasted time and energy.

Existing Provision
It could be a misuse of resources if a parish contemplates any kind of provision for young people when the same or a similar type of service is already being offered locally. This may seem obvious, but all too frequently a church struggles to provide, say, an open youth club when only a few hundred yards away the same kind of provision is being offered by another organization (the local education authority perhaps) with greater resources of cash and manpower. In this situation the parish would do better to identify an alternative need and aim to supply something different. A drama club, a football club, or an advice centre may be what is needed, or the church may decide to concentrate all its resources on work with its own younger members.

Sometimes it might be best for members of the congregation who have a concern for the young to amalgamate with those already working elsewhere in the locality, or to assist at another church in an area where little is already being done. The latter suggestion presupposes, however, a breadth of vision that goes beyond parish boundaries, and sadly this is often lacking.

The 'Clients'

Having examined what is already available in the area, the parish should look closely at the 'clients' – the young people for whom they wish to make some kind of provision. It is easy for adults to assume that they know how young people are thinking, what they want and what they enjoy. It is also easy for adults to instigate activities which really only reflect their own interests either at the present moment or when they themselves were young.

The first method of assessing the 'clientele' is inevitably *observation*. Each adult will have observed local young people even if unconsciously, and may have children of his or her own. The problem here is the same as with any unscientific survey; one might have noticed, or remembered, only young people of a particular sort. An act of vandalism is likely to stick in the mind far more than the impression created by a dozen well-behaved young people. Likewise, the fact that one's own daughter likes horse riding and sewing does not mean that all young women do. It is also possible to draw misleading conclusions from observations. Vandalism may be caused by boredom, by a bad home background, by an evil nature, or any combination of causes. Pure observation of an act of vandalism is unlikely to give all the information required to identify the needs of that particular group of young people. Observation may give some useful starting points but they need to be confirmed or otherwise by additional means.

There are two main ways of obtaining the accurate information needed; interviews and questionnaires.

Interviews can be a one-to-one process, as when somebody goes out onto the streets, or from door to door, with a set of questions, or they can be done in a group, with all the young people present joining in with thoughts and comments, and notes being kept of important things which are said. The advantages of interviews are that the questioner can add any additional enquiries that seem necessary, he can ask for clarification if he does not fully understand the answers, he can alter questions if they are not understood, and can re-state ones which are being avoided. But there are disadvantages. The young people may change because of the presence of the interviewer and give the answers they think are required. Little time is available for responding to questions and the 'spur of the moment' comment may not be the most truthful and exact. And the notes made by the interviewer might be coloured by his own preconceived ideas and not reflect exactly what was said. *Questionnaires* have the advantage of anonymity and they give the young people time to think before answering. On the other hand the questions have to be worded very carefully and even then can be misunderstood, and no possibility exists to press for a fuller or clearer answer. Each parish must decide which method is most appropriate in its own situation, or might opt for a combination of the two. But whatever is decided it is important that a thorough attempt is made to identify the needs and interests of the young people one hopes to serve.

Staff

After examining the young people, one needs next to look at potential staff and their skills. Given the expressed needs of the young people, *how many* adults are available who could, with training if necessary, attempt to meet those needs? What is their *motivation* – why do they want to be involved: do they really have the well-being of the young people at heart? What is their level of *commitment* – will they support the venture in difficult times; are their lives so committed already that other things may turn them aside after a short time (young people frequently need a lengthy period to cement a relationship with adults)?

What do the adults themselves want to achieve in their work with the young – do these aims coincide with the aim of the project, or will there be pressure from the staff to deviate from the original purpose? Even if the staff have a general concern for the young, do they possess the *skills* that are required in the proposed venture, and do the skills of the individuals complement each other in such a way that the team as a whole has all those required? What are the *relationships* like between the adults – will they work together as a team, will they function best with a strong leader (and who?) or as a collective? These are the sort of questions to which carefully considered answers are necessary. Insufficient staff, ones of the wrong kind, or ones who do not work well together, can effectively destroy even the most carefully planned piece of youth work.

Most of the information about potential staff will be obtained from existing personal knowledge, but in some situations interviews will be appropriate (see p. 19f). Except when making a formal application for a job, people, especially church members, have a great reluctance to admit to the skills they possess. One simple method which helps to identify them, and which can be used in a small group situation, is to give every person a sheet of paper and ask them to write on it two or three things they are good at and two or three things they are not so good at, or indeed find impossible. These things could be related to any specific area of youth work being contemplated. So, if open club work is envisaged, one person might feel she would be good at helping with the canteen, doing craft work and any musical activity, but think she should be avoided when someone is needed to organize football, exercise discipline or do home visits. Similarly if an advice centre is proposed, one adult might have the skills to give legal advice and to help with problems concerning employment and unemployment, but feel incapable of doing secretarial and administrative work.

Asking for details of those areas where individuals feel deficient (or unable to help through lack of time) not only produces important and useful information but also makes people feel better about acknowledging their strengths.

Resources

The next information required to make a well-informed decision about a new venture concerns resources. In most fields of youth work the main material resource will be a *building* where the activity can take place. The existence or absence of suitable premises is obviously as crucial to a venture as is the availability of staff. Again fairly obviously, the size of the building may help determine the provision offered. In the absence of a sufficiently large hall which can accommodate ball games, catering facilities and craft work, and also offers lavatories, small rooms for group work and an office, large scale open youth work will be impossible. In addition other uses of the building may limit its youth work potential. If it is already used by a lunch club for the elderly or as a dining hall for a local school, then day-time provision for the young unemployed would not be possible. Again, if used by uniformed organizations two nights a week, by a playgroup in the mornings and the Mothers' Union on Thursday afternoons, equipment which cannot easily be packed away such as carpentry benches, photographic developing equipment and heavy pool tables, will be out of the question.

Nearness and accessibility are two other factors to be considered. If, for example, the target group for the new provision is the young people on a certain estate then careful consideration must be given to how readily they would go to a building if it were out of their area. Noting their existing habits of movement and travel will give some indication of mobility. The problem is especially acute in village communities too. Young people may be reluctant to travel to the next village or neighbouring town (or their parents be reluctant to let them) even if transport is provided. But nearness does not always equate with accessibility. Railway lines and busy roads can form barriers which prevent young people travelling to a venue only a short distance from home. Less obvious barriers exist as well. Habitual travel from home only in one direction to school, shops and bus stop may may mean that nearby streets and buildings in another direction are unknown; and the unfamiliar can be daunting.

After buildings, the most important material resource is *finance*. As Jesus reminds us in a more profound context, nobody undertakes a new venture without first sitting down and counting the cost. The kind of questions that need consideration are, what will it cost to rent (or buy) the premises, what will be the running costs for electricity, heating, telephone, insurance and regular redecoration and repairs; will cleaning have to be paid for, how much will equipment cost, not just at the start but remembering consumable items, and will any staff be paid and at what rate? Having worked out expenditure, attention needs to be given to income; how much will each young person contribute, how much will be expected from the sponsoring body, will the local education authority help, and are there charitable sources? As Mr Micawber reminds us, 'Annual income twenty pounds, annual expenditure nineteen nineteen six, result happiness. Annual income twenty pounds, annual expenditure twenty pounds ought and six, result misery'.

The Decision

Only after assessing existing local provision, the 'clients', the possible staff and the resources can a decision be sensibly made about what kind of activity to provide. The answer may be that there is nothing the parish can do in the situation that would meet the young people's needs, and it is better to admit it than to waste time and effort in masterminding a flop.

Deciding to provide some kind of youth facility is not everything: its duration should also be determined. It is not

necessary, nor always prudent, to start a project of indeter-
minate length, though this is quite justified if it is a conscious
and well-reasoned decision. But sometimes a definite finishing date is appropriate as, for example, when premises are
short-life, when staff can commit themselves only for a
period, when funding is limited, or when the venture is
designed to meet a transient need. Staff should know from
the outset what their commitment is likely to be.

Publicity

Once the decision is made, the question of publicity will need
attention. How will young people hear about what is being
offered? Will they hear by word of mouth or is something else
needed? This could take the form of handbills delivered door
to door by parishioners, or distributed to schools, or in the
shopping centre. Alternatively, posters could be displayed on
noticeboards and in shop and house windows. An advert in
the parish magazine or in the local paper may also be
appropriate. Much will depend on the kind of area and the
type of activity offered.

Particular care is needed in advertising young people's
advice centres. The success of the whole venture depends on
the service's existence being known to potential clientele, so
in addition to leaflets and posters it is essential that key
people in the community know about it; these will include
the police, doctors, other clergy, and youth workers in
neighbouring clubs.

Posters and handbills will have to compete with the high-
budget productions of commercial organizations which
readily capture young people's attention. It is unlikely that
money will be to hand for anything lavish, but without
excessive expenditure even a one colour item can express
vitality and evoke young people's interest. The use of a lay-
out artist or the design section of a printers can pay off: it
would be unfortunate if a good venture was let down by
second-rate publicity.

Review

Finally, however good the groundwork for a new venture it is still possible to make mistakes, but a regular review of how well the original intention is standing up in the light of experience can ensure mistakes are not perpetuated. It is also crucial to remember that young people change rapidly. Provision that meets their needs today may be unnecessary or unwanted tomorrow. And new needs arise from time to time. Staff also change; they lose enthusiasm for activities they once enjoyed and conversely develop additional skills which may enable new work to be tried.

Conclusion

The thought of undertaking the above process of investigation and evaluation may be daunting. A new venture may get off the ground successfully without it, but experience suggests that the greatest chance of meeting young people's needs follows from thorough investigation and careful planning. And it is only the venture that meets their needs which can claim to be a success.

Chapter 8

Residential Events

It is possible to achieve more with a group of young people in one residential weekend than in a year of one-night-a-week sessions, but many are the pitfalls which can make a disaster out of a potential success.

Most youth clubs or church choirs choose to go away independently, but residential events are, of course, organized centrally by groups such as Pathfinders, The Royal School of Church Music, The National Trust, The British Council of Churches and individual dioceses. (Addresses can be found in Appendix 5.) These are particularly useful where a church has insufficient young people to make a viable residential event of its own, or where specialist training or activities are sought. Even if there are enough young people locally for an event of their own, much can be gained by encouraging them to take part in activities which extend beyond the parish group.

The Aim
Clearly establish the aim of the residential event before planning anything else. Decide whether the young people want a specialist activity event, e.g. pony trekking, sailing, or nature conservancy; whether it is to be purely recreational, or an 'educational' time during which participants will study a topic such as peace, the problem of evil, the Holy Week stories, love, fellowship, or creation, or a mixture of both

recreation and 'education'. If you intend to undertake a specialist activity it is absolutely essential that suitably qualified instructors/supervisors are available.

From the aim develop a series of objectives – the detailed activities which will help achieve the aim. If the aim is to explore 'love', then the activities might include a film or video about caring for young homeless children, a Bible study on God's love for humanity, learning two new Christian songs on the theme of love, devising a piece of dance-drama on the same theme, and making a collage of magazine pictures showing love. Anything which does not fit the aim, however attractive in itself, should be rejected.

Ensure at the beginning that the young people who will participate are involved in planning: it is pointless arranging an event only to find it does not appeal to them. Similarly all the adults taking part in the residential event should be involved with planning from its inception, only then will it have their wholehearted support. For a mixed group there should always be at least one staff member of each sex.

The Venue
The venue will be determined by a number of factors. First it must offer facilities that enable you to do the activities you want, e.g. sufficient space for effective small group work. The cost must be considered too. Travelling more than thirty or forty miles, especially if going away for only a weekend, is likely to over-inflate the total cost, though this will depend on the kind of transport used. Careful costing is essential.

A decision needs to be made about whether to use self-catering accommodation or somewhere where all the cooking and domestic chores are done for you. The latter will be more expensive but will leave the group extra time for other activities. If however the aim is to build the group together more closely then the corporate act of preparing and cooking food can be an asset. Again, cost may determine whether you opt for self-catering. Bear in mind the financial resources and family background of the group when choosing the venue. Some will feel at home in very basic accommodation while others will naturally expect higher standards of comfort and have the money to pay for it.

Decide too on whether you want a country or city venue. This may be determined by your aim, and also by the parish from which the group comes. Usually one thinks of residential events happening in the country, but young people from a country parish may find a city venue more exciting and stimulating.

Your diocese may have a residential centre of its own for young people. Failing that, the Diocesan Youth Officer should be able to supply a list of centres. (See also: *Holiday and Conference Centre Guide* which contains details of over 550 conference centres, holiday houses and camp sites for young people, together with lists of agencies which organize holidays and other residential events. Available from the National Youth Bureau (address on p. 148). Even this comprehensive work does not include everything available.) The best places tend to get fully booked months in advance so early preparation is essential. Adult workers should visit beforehand to see exactly what facilities are available, making a particular note of what equipment is provided and what will have to be taken from home, of whether the sleeping arrangements limit the proportion of each sex, and other crucial matters such as the type of electric sockets and whether they are conveniently situated. Find out also where and when payment has to be made, so you can obtain a cheque from the parish treasurer in advance if necessary.

Insurance cover for any trip away from the home base is essential. On this see the section on insurance in Chapter 4.

The Letter Home

Once all the arrangements have been made a letter should be prepared for prospective participants and their parents. It should give the venue, the dates, the time of departure and arrival back, the cost (a note saying that some funds may be available to help if necessary may enable an unemployed young person or the child of a poorer family to attend), and an outline of the proposed activities (this is particularly important where hazardous events are planned).

Attached to the letter should be a returnable application form. The example below includes the details usually required but local conditions may demand additional items.

Application Form for St Mark's Youth Club Weekend at
The Granary, Bletchingley, Surrey
Friday 27 to Sunday 29 April 1984

Name ....

Address ....

....

Telephone Number .... Age ....

Any medical conditions of which the staff should know, e.g. epilepsy

....

I agree to .... (Name)
attending the St Mark's Youth Club Weekend 27–29 April 1984. I enclose a non-returnable deposit of £5 and agree to pay the balance of £6.50 on or before 27 April.

Signed ....
(Parent/Guardian for those under 18)

Return to the Revd G. Smith, The Vicarage, Church Lane, by 1 March 1984

The date for returning the form will depend on how long in advance the conference centre or camp site needs to know numbers.

The initial letter should be followed by a second one after all the applications are received confirming (or otherwise) that the applicant has a place, listing kit to be taken (e.g.

sleeping bag, towel, note book, washing kit, at least one complete change of clothes, walking shoes, swimming costume, etc.), and giving complete details of time and place for departure and return. Also give the telephone number and address of the residential centre. A reminder about the fee still to be paid may not go amiss.

The Programme

As well as adhering to the pre-determined theme, the programme must be full, interesting, varied and appropriate; full because a programme which allows too much free time encourages the young people to find activities of their own devising, and there is a reasonable chance that these will be disruptive or destructive. The troublesome group is nearly always a bored group. For much the same reason the programme should be interesting and varied. A whole weekend spent in discussion groups is unlikely to elicit a constructive response from participants. And even a diet of films palls after a while. A wide range of learning techniques exists. These include drama, dance, art, music, quizzes, educational games, short talks (to be used very sparingly), discussion, film, video, slides, role play, visits, Bible study, worksheets, and much more beside (see Chapter 6). Those who plan programmes need to be as imaginative as possible. And the programme should be appropriate to the group, bearing in mind their age, sex, educational ability, and natural interests. It may be stating the obvious to say that a group of bright eighteen-year-olds need a different approach from a group of not-so-bright fourteen-year-olds, but all too often the style of programme is determined by the adults' interests rather than by close attention to what is best for the young people. Work out in advance every detail of the programme. Decide which staff member is responsible for what, and list all the equipment and materials you will need and ensure that someone is clearly given responsibility for bringing them. The absence of so small an item as a box of felt pens can ruin a well-planned programme.

Set out below is a typical programme for a residential weekend for a group of mixed sex and ability. If it were a self-catering event then time would be allocated for food preparation. The supposed age range is wide, so provision is made for some of the work to be done in small groups which can cater for this. It is only an example; not a blueprint from which no one should deviate.

PROGRAMME

THEME: What has Christianity to say to the world in which we live?

FRIDAY	5.00 p.m.	Staff arrive
	6.15–6.45 p.m.	Young people arrive
	7.00 p.m.	Supper
	8.00–9.30 p.m.	Announcements and notices
		Introductory games – getting to know each other better
	9.30 p.m.	Evening worship
	10.00 p.m.	Evening drink
	11.00 p.m.	Lights out
SATURDAY	8.30 a.m.	Breakfast
	9.30 a.m.	Worship
	9.45 a.m.	WHO IS DIFFERENT? Ethnic minorities and others
		Film: New Ways (12 mins) about the problems faced by Asians settling into a new community. Discussion in small groups

10.45 a.m.	Coffee
11.15 a.m.	WORKSHOPS on the theme: Christ and the World Drama, Dance, Music and Art
1.00 p.m.	Lunch
1.30 p.m.	Free time (Country walk for anyone interested.)
3.00 p.m.	WHO HAS WHAT? The rich and the poor USPG filmstrip, plus work on project pack
4.00 p.m.	Tea
4.30 p.m.	WHO HAS WHAT? cont.
5.30 p.m.	IS WORK EVERYTHING? Employment and Unemployment. Short introductory talk. Bible study in small groups: Why is a person valuable?
7.00 p.m.	Supper
8.00 p.m.	Party (including production by the revue group Sold Out)
11.00 p.m.	Lights out

SUNDAY	8.30 a.m.	Breakfast
	9.30 a.m.	WAR AND PEACE Violence Educational Game: 'Starpower'
	10.45 a.m.	Coffee
	11.15 a.m.	Discussion in small groups
	12.15 p.m.	Preparation for worship
	1.00 p.m.	Lunch

| 3.00 p.m. | Holy Communion (including presentations from the discussion and workshop groups) |
| 4.00 p.m. | Tea and depart |

Particular attention needs to be given to the start of an event. Participants may be apprehensive, feel isolated from the rest of the group, and be tired after a week of school or work. Adults should be sufficiently organized in advance so that they are free to welcome the young people as they arrive, to show them where they are sleeping, and perhaps to give them a cup of tea. The programme on the first night should be as light as possible.

Tell the young people the outline of the weekend: knowing what is to happen helps allay fears. Likewise clearly state rules about lights-out, smoking, punctuality and so forth. If staying in a centre that has a warden, he or she should be given an opportunity early on to welcome and talk to the group.

During the residential period the adults will be under constant scrutiny. More important than what they say will be the way they behave. For example, the adult who misses a session so he can go to the shops or the pub says an enormous amount about the value of the session he is missing.

Some free time is essential and usually much valued by the group, especially by those with weekend homework. But this is not necessarily free time for the staff. Adults should be available to talk to individuals or small groups, to ensure good behaviour and to suggest activities to the less imaginative.

One of the greatest indications of a good teacher is the ability to 'plan on one's feet'. However carefully a residential event is organized, last minute adaptations will almost certainly be necessary in order to respond to an obvious need in the group, because an item finishes earlier than expected or because the weather prohibits a planned activity. Adults should have extra items up their sleeves, and should be prepared to forsake even the most brilliant activity should circumstances demand it.

In the course of even a weekend, a group takes on an identity of its own, and the introduction of an outsider late on in the life of a group can drastically alter its nature. So think carefully before inviting your vicar to join you for Saturday supper, or before asking the local curate to celebrate Communion on Sunday. Similarly both young people and adults should be discouraged from leaving early: this too can destroy a group's identity.

What happens at bedtime is usually the source of more trouble to a group than anything else. The lights-out time should be decided on with reference to the age of the group members. It is most likely to be adhered to when the participants themselves have a say in deciding the time. This could be a topic for discussion on the first evening, though the adults may need to contribute an element of realism! Whilst the staff should expect late night talking and perambulations, they still need to enforce the rules justly and firmly. Only this way will they get any sleep at all. A residential event lasting longer than a weekend usually settles down after a couple of nights – with the definite exception of the night before going home. A quiet activity such as reading a story or late evening worship may help to settle a group.

How an event ends is almost as important as what happens during it. Leaving a group which has been friendly, supportive and enjoyable can be almost a bereavement in miniature. Time should be allowed for good-byes either at the centre or, if travelling together, on arrival at the home base. And adults should make themselves available for their part in the proceedings, and not be dashing around clearing up and dealing with their own personal arrangements. Arranging a reunion on a specified date in the future can help to lessen the feeling of loss.

Food

Good quality food can contribute greatly to the enjoyment of a residential event. If you have the chance of sampling a meal at a centre before booking to go there, then certainly take the opportunity. There is no need for unappetizing, over-cooked and unimaginative food. Even with the lowest of budgets, flair and imagination can achieve much, and centres that offer poor food are best avoided.

If you are catering for yourselves then you have only yourselves to blame if you end up with 'twelve great basketfuls' of unwanted food. If the planning group for your residential event lacks anyone with skill in bulk catering there may be someone in the congregation who will advise. Guiders often prove especially useful in this area. Plan each meal carefully to give a balanced menu, and always have eggs, cheese, bread and fruit secretly in reserve for those who really do not like a particular meal.

List separately every ingredient necessary for each meal in order to make a complete list of all your needs. Add to the list supplementary items such as pepper, salt and cooking oil. Even though laborious, a costing as exact as possible should be made early on so that participants can be charged at a realistic level. Decide which items can best be bought in advance (from a large supermarket or cash and carry) and which are better obtained fresh at local shops (if any).

The equipment available at the residential centre may determine your menus. Find out in advance if there is a fridge or a freezer, and what cooking and eating utensils are available (boiled eggs without eggcups can be painful on the fingers unless you were a Boy Scout and know how to improvise with a hole in a thick slice of bread!). Members of the parish not directly involved with the event may enjoy helping by cooking food in advance.

Below is a sample menu for a weekend with fifteen participants. Costings have not been included as prices change so rapidly.

Friday		*Shopping needs:*
Supper	Steak & Kidney Pie	3 large Steak &
	Creamed Potatoes	Kidney Pies (cooked
	Carrots	by members of the
	Fresh Fruit	parish)
	Tea or Coffee	Large pack of Instant
		Potato
		2lb Frozen Carrots
		15 Apples
		2 pints Milk
Late Drink	Tea, Coffee, Biscuits	3 pints Milk
		2 packets Biscuits

Saturday		
Breakfast	Cereals	5 pints Milk, Cereal
	Sausages & Tomatoes	30 Sausages
	Toast & Marmalade	30 Tomatoes
	Tea or Coffee	2 loaves (1 brown, 1 white)
Lunch (picnic)	Cheese & Tomato Sandwiches	1lb Cheese
		15 Tomatoes
	Paté Sandwiches	4 packets Paté
	Crisps	15 packets Crisps
	Fruit	15 Oranges &
	Ready-made orange	Bananas
		8 pints diluted Orange Squash
Tea	Tea & Cakes	Cakes (made by parishioners)
Supper	Spaghetti Bolognaise	2lbs Spaghetti
	Rhubarb Crumble	Oxo cubes
	Tea or Coffee	1lb Onions
		4lb Mince
		1 large tin of Tomatoes

		2 tins Rhubarb
		Crumble Mix
		2 pints Milk

| Late drink | Tea, Coffee, Chocolate Biscuits | 3 pints Milk 2 packets Biscuits |

Sunday

| Breakfast | Cereals
Boiled Eggs
Toast & Marmalade
Tea or Coffee | Cereal
5 pints Milk
15 Eggs
2 loaves (1 brown, 1 white) |

| Lunch | Roast Turkey
Roast Potatoes
Peas
Stuffing
Tinned Fruit & Ice Cream
Tea or Coffee | 3 Turkey Roasts
5lb Potatoes
2lb frozen Peas
1 packet stuffing
2 large tins of Mixed Fruit
1 litre Ice Cream
2 pints Milk |

General shopping

| | Pepper
Salt
Cooking Oil
Marmalade and Jam
4 packets assorted Cereals
Polythene sacks for rubbish
Washing up Liquid | 200g Instant Coffee
60 Tea Bags
Small tin Chocolate
2kg Sugar
Polythene lunch bags
Dish cloths
Tea Towels |

Problems

Discipline during a residential event is important so that good relationships are preserved with those who run the centre and with neighbours, and so that no participant is prevented from enjoying himself by the actions of another.

Disruptive members should be disciplined immediately and before a pattern of bad behaviour becomes established. As a last resort a young person could be banned from future events or sent home at once. The chief antidote to disruptive behaviour is an enjoyable and energy-consuming programme; this should decrease the need for excessive discipline. One reason for bad behaviour may be a desire for attention. In my experience the attention seeker, whether he exhibits bad behaviour, refuses to eat at meal-times or whatever, is best ignored (if possible) while the attention seeking acts are happening, but should be given additional care and attention in between.

Adult staff must be prepared to deal with injury and sickness should they occur. Ideally at least one member of staff should have first aid experience, and this is essential when hazardous pursuits are undertaken. They should be equipped with basic first aid supplies, and a bottle of pain killers usually proves useful to remedy headaches. It is also well worth being prepared for the young women who is totally taken by surprise by the onset of a period.

Whether to allow participants to drink alcohol either at the centre or in a local pub is a difficult decision particularly with a group with a wide age range. The law says that young people under fourteen are not allowed in bars during drinking hours, but those between the ages of fourteen and eighteen can enter a bar but only to consume non-alcoholic drink. It is only illegal to drink alcohol elsewhere if the person is under five years old, so consuming it at the centre will be at the discretion of the staff (or warden if there is one). Much will depend on the age of the group and whether members are likely to be allowed to drink at home. As a general rule for groups with at least some members under eighteen it is best to outlaw alcohol, though few parents are likely to object if their son or daughter is offered a glass of wine or cider with, say, Sunday lunch.

Evaluation

To avoid perpetuating bad elements in a residential event and in order to build on strengths, some evaluation is necessary at the end. Participants can be involved with this either by discussion or by filling in a 'reaction sheet'. This can be done as the last session of the event, or at a later date, perhaps at a regular club meeting. Below is a form of questionnaire which can be adapted to suit many types of event. How much participants have enjoyed an item is important, not least because learning is best done when enjoyment is present.

EVALUATION SHEET

Name ....

(You may hope for more honest comments if anonymity is preserved.)

1. How have you found the programme?

    | interesting | boring |
    | useful | anger-producing |
    | helpful | irritating |
    | friendly | unproductive |
    | worthwhile | uncomfortable |

    Tick the words you agree with

2. How did you find the session on ....?

    Useful |___|___|___|___|___| Not useful

    Enjoyable |___|___|___|___|___| Not enjoyable

    [This example can be repeated for each session]

3. Write down three things you liked about the programme.

4. Write down three things you disliked about the programme.

5. Have you any suggestions for making future programmes better?

6. Are there topics you would like to spend more time on?

In addition to the evaluation by participants, staff should meet together after the event to make their own assessment. Ideally a record should be made of strengths and weaknesses for reference when the next one is being planned.

Residential events are hard work and take considerable time to plan, but all this is far outweighed by their value.

Chapter 9

Special Topics

This chapter contains brief notes on a variety of topics associated with church youth work. The brevity demanded by lack of space is hopefully counteracted by references, wherever possible, for further reading.

Scouts and Guides
Both Scouts and Guides have their own headquarters staff which provide a back-up service of information, training and general assistance. For this reason less demand tends to be made on the local church to provide support, even for sponsored groups. Unfortunately this can lead to isolation unless there is a determined effort on the part of church members to incorporate the groups into the mainstream life of the Christian community.

The stresses and strains which exist all too often between clergy and church members on the one hand and leaders of uniformed organizations on the other would usually be diminished if better communication existed between the two, and each understood the other's aims and objectives and their methods for achieving them. Most uniformed organizations produce leaflets explaining their work (e.g. the Scouts issue *The Religious Policy of Scouting*. For address see Appendix 5). An occasional exhibition in church of the work of uniformed organizations helps to incorporate them into the church, as does their offering to help with parish activities.

Parade services present perennial problems. Should uniformed organizations attend the regular Parish Communion or should they have special services of their own? If they come to the usual Sunday morning service, to what extent should they be allowed to dominate it? My own view starts by asking what will benefit the young people most, and the most common answer is a service of their own, in which they participate as fully as possible and which has a strong emphasis on lively teaching. But this is not a perfect answer and arrangements will depend on local circumstances.

Handicapped Young People

The feeling still exists that separate provision, beyond the capability and skills of the average church, are required by the handicapped. In some cases this is true, but with a general move in education circles to integrate the handicapped wherever possible, churches need to ask if and how they might be able to help. The informal and flexible way in which the youth service functions means that there is more chance of integrating handicapped young people there than in the more formal school environment.

If a church wants to explore the possibilities, the first task is to ascertain what provision, if any, exists elsewhere in the locality. Existing groups may welcome the offer of premises for their activities or be prepared to provide experienced personnel to advise on the setting up of new ventures. Unless suitable expertise exists already in the Christian community it may also be useful to liaise, as appropriate, with one of the many national organizations such as the Royal National Institute for the Blind, MENCAP, and PHAB.

If there is a commitment to make provision for handicapped young people then a church will need to give attention to four main points. First, *access*. Physically handicapped young people can only attend club activities if they can gain access to the building. This is not always possible unless alterations are made.

The second point that needs to be considered is *transport*. Severely handicapped young people, including those with a visual handicap, may be incapable of attending a youth club unless transport is provided. It may be impossible for them to use public transport, and relatives may have no vehicle of their own or may not be free to leave other children at home to escort the handicapped young person to and from a club.

Third, attention needs to be given to *training*. Workers need an understanding of the handicaps which their young people have. They must understand their limitations and their potential. Training opportunities may be offered by national or local organizations, by the local education authority, or may take place 'on the job' through the assistance of personnel from other local groups. Work with handicapped young people is very demanding and a decision to instigate or be involved with such work must include a commitment to training.

Lastly, and perhaps obviously, care is needed in constructing the youth club *programme*. Its nature will vary according to the clientele, whether they are both handicapped and able-bodied, or just handicapped, and on the nature of the handicaps.

As much as providing learning and growing opportunities for the disabled, an integrated youth club catering for able-bodied young people as well, helps them develop a healthy attitude towards the disabled. Too many myths and fears about disability still exist. Such clubs, and indeed other integrated activities, can be growth points not just for the handicapped but for the able-bodied young person too.

Working with Girls

The traditional roles of girls and young women in society have been challenged in recent years. There is a real concern that young women are cast in a 'domestic' mould whether that is what they want or not. When educating girls, either in school or youth club, it is important that they have the greatest number of choices open to them at the end of the day. Their potential is diminished if they are encouraged only to think in terms of marriage, child-rearing and housework. For some this will be exactly what they want to do, but some will have the aptitude and inclination to do different things, and a third group will only realize the alternatives if someone shows them the full range of opportunities.

What then can be done in church and youth club to help young women identify and fulfil their God-given potential?
1. Staff should ideally be an equal mix of males and females. Unless girls see women in leadership roles they are likely to learn by experience that men naturally assume such positions.
2. In mixed clubs girls should have the same range of activities open to them as do the boys. It should not be assumed that boys will play football while girls do cooking.
3. Boys tend to exclude girls from activities. It is important that girls have a fair chance to take part in all club activities.
4. Girls often welcome the opportunity to meet together without boys. (Those who want only to be around the boys have already adopted a traditional female role.) In practical terms there could be a club night just for girls or a girls-only room in the club premises.
5. Much advertising and many films and television programmes proclaim a very limited female role. Time could be given to helping girls understand this and encouraging them to see the alternatives.
6. In both church and youth club girls need opportunities to be involved with decision making as much as the boys.
7. When recruiting for church jobs it should not be assumed that girls will do the domestic chores.

Unemployment
Unemployment means wasted skills, a decrease in self-esteem, and sometimes an increase in physical and mental

illness, to say nothing of its wider effect on the economy and the community. It is likely to continue an important topic for many young people.

At a basic level, churches can provide the personnel who can get alongside individual young people to support and encourage them during unemployment. Some churches have also used their premises as 'drop-in centres' where young people can call to get advice over a cup of coffee on job vacancies and applications – help with form-filling, letter writing and phone calls. But with the steady decrease in job opportunities youth workers are moving away from this kind of approach towards one which helps young people to come to terms with the prospect of no employment at all. This work mainly takes place with individuals and small groups, and centres on discussing and demonstrating the value life has without paid employment. It also encourages constructive use of enforced leisure time and tries to prevent the despondency which so often accompanies lack of work.

One constructive form of action a local church can take is to sponsor or otherwise be involved with a Manpower Services Commission scheme. Their new venture, called the *Youth Training Scheme* aims ultimately to give all young people under eighteen, who have finished full-time education, the opportunity to undertake a year of work experience, education and training. It is open to men and women. The majority of places are provided by commercial employers but some are expected to be sponsored by community projects, churches and the like. In the past young people have been involved with decoration and restoration of church buildings, halls and churchyards, with workshops set up on church premises, even as trainee vergers.

The scheme is a complicated one and it is beyond the space available here to explain it in full. Details can be obtained from Manpower Services Commission Area Offices (addresses in telephone directories). The National Youth Bureau publishes a number of useful booklets on work with the young unemployed (address – Appendix 5). But beware,

however concerned a church is to help the young unemployed it should not undertake involvement with an MSC
scheme without first sitting down and counting the cost.
Further Reading: *The Christian and Unemployment*, Wendy
Green (Mowbray, 1982).

Drugs and Glue

The non-medical use of drugs (cannabis, LSD, tranquillizers,
amphetamines and barbiturates) and the inhalation of
solvents (impact adhesives, butane gas, aerosol propellants,
paint thinners, nail-polish removers, etc.) are the cause of
considerable concern. But what is acceptable to society and
what is not varies from place to place and from age to age.
Opium was once widely used and freely available in
England: it is now strictly controlled. Alcohol, outlawed by
some cultures, is readily obtainable, yet like tobacco, can be
addictive, cause lasting physical damage, and can kill.

The cultural mix in British society creates tensions. Young
Rastafarians, for example, will point to biblical texts such as
'the earth brought forth grass and herb yielding seed . . . and
God saw that it was good' (Genesis 1.11–12), and thereby
justify their use of ganja (cannabis). To them it is almost
sacramental. At the same time they may deride alcohol as
destructive. Without permitting illegal practices, the youth
worker must be aware of differing cultural views about some
drugs.

The common causes of solvent-sniffing or drug-taking are
curiosity, boredom, the influence of friends and the avoid-
ance of problems and anxieties.

Youth workers can help in a preventative way by
providing education about the effects of drugs, including
alcohol and tobacco: most young people are pitifully
ignorant. They can also help by supplying 'crisis information'
informally or through an advice centre. When confronted by
a young person under the influence of drugs or solvents the
method will depend on the symptoms; he will be firm yet

understanding with the over-active, supportive and comforting with the depressed (depression is just as devastating whether caused by drugs, alcohol or 'natural' causes), and tolerant and calmly accepting with the one who is hallucinating and suffering a 'bad trip'. Those who have become very sleepy need urgent medical attention to prevent irreversible coma, and those who have been on stimulants but are now experiencing severe depression need constant attention lest suicide follows.

As far as possible drug users and solvent sniffers should be treated as normal. Illegal substances should *not* be allowed on club premises, nor should the use of solvents, but it is best not to exclude known users, first because this leads to alienation, second because those thus ostracized will seek out alternative places in which to spend their time, and derelict houses and similar venues can be extremely dangerous to those whose perception is unbalanced, and thirdly because those removed from the club may also be removed from possible help and understanding. Further Reading: *Youth in Society* No. 68 (National Youth Bureau). See also publications issued by organizations listed under Health Education in Appendix 3.

Advising on the Law
From time to time workers with the young will be faced with problems which contain a legal element. They could come in the form of direct questions or could arise from their behaviour. The most important thing is to know one's own limitations and never to give advice unless one hundred per cent certain of the facts. In many circumstances it will be necessary to admit ignorance but at the same time to know where professional knowledge can be sought – from a Citizens' Advice Bureau, a law centre, or from a friendly solicitor. Useful handbooks are also available about young people and the law, but it must be remembered that English law is constantly developing so information may be out of

date. Except in the simplest cases it is best to refer young people to the professionals, but bearing in mind that this could be a daunting prospect for some young people, and they may need an adult in whom they have confidence to be an intermediary or to accompany them to an interview.

Some basic legal facts are outlined below:

1. No one under ten can be arrested.

2. Anyone can be searched by the police if they have previously been arrested. Even without arresting a person the police can search for drugs, firearms, sometimes for stolen goods, or if they suspect an involvement with terrorism.

3. No child under ten can be charged with a criminal offence. Young people aged between ten and thirteen can only be convicted of a criminal offence if it can be shown that they understood that their actions were wrong. Someone fourteen or over is considered fully responsible. No lower age limit exists for civil wrongs such as libel, assault and trespass but young people must be shown to have understood the nature of their actions.

4. A young person can, at the discretion of the judge, be a witness at any age.

5. If necessary a young person of any age can see a solicitor.

6. Except with a licence for public performing no one can work until they are thirteen. Between thirteen and sixteen employment is restricted by various national and local regulations. The local education authority can provide details. Earnings belong to the young person, not to his parents.

7. No one can marry until they are sixteen, and consent of their parents or a court is needed if they wish to marry under eighteen. Once married their parents have no legal authority over them.

8. Those over fourteen can enter a pub, but until eighteen can only consume soft drinks.

9. A girl under sixteen may not consent to sexual intercourse. No such restriction exists for boys.

10. There are no age restrictions on smoking in private, but if seen in public a young person may have his tobacco confiscated by the police. It is an offence to sell tobacco to anyone who looks under sixteen even if not for their own use. Further Reading: *Under 18* – a guide to the law as it affects young people, National Youth Bureau (for address see Appendix 5); *The Penguin Guide to the Law*, John Pritchard (Penguin Books Ltd, 1982).

Political Education

For over a decade, at least some educationalists have pressed for political education in schools. They have recognized the need for young people who live in a democracy to be politically aware and active: to know about local and central government, to be critical of political opinions, and to know how to influence decision making. Only dictators hope to limit political education. Youth groups too have been identified as places where political education can take place. If we believe God is concerned about men, women and children, about the quality of their lives, about their health, their housing and their education (all areas in which the Church has been involved for centuries) then political education is a crucial subject for Christians. They will especially be concerned to look at the theological and moral dimension of political decisions.

Some people, Christians and non-Christians alike, avoid political education because they see it as something theoretical and intellectually over-demanding. Certainly it can be approached as an academic subject, but in the youth group it is most likely to be dealt with very practically. A dispute over the fairness of someone's action, in for example a football match, can lead to a simple discussion on Justice. When Delroy has his bike stolen there is an opportunity to think about the need for laws; if Linda cannot get a job, then discuss what causes unemployment; and the night Gavin arrives clutching two South African oranges there could be the chance to explore the pros and cons of supporting the economy of a country which advocates apartheid. The skilled and sensitive youth worker will take whatever opportunities are available to help equip young people for life in today's society, and where appropriate will explore what Christianity has to say to a particular situation. The Christian youth worker will not always find political education easy, in fact at times he or she will have to do some very hard thinking indeed, but if we believe it important to take Christian insights into the life of the world then to attempt it is important. Further reading: *Political Education*, A Practical Guide for Christian Youth Workers, Fred Milson (The Paternoster Press, 1980).

Peace Education

Many young people demonstrate the attraction of war and violence by avidly reading war comics and by watching violent films and videos. The Church has an important role in extolling the virtues of peace. It should also help young people think through the pros and cons of nuclear weapons.

Young people will have experienced lack of peace in their own relationships with neighbours, friends and family. So this will probably be the starting point for learning. The youth worker will begin where the young people are and help them reflect on what destroys peace in their own relationships. Next he will help them examine whether the factors which create discord within nations and between nations have the same kind of origin. Always the question will be asked: What could have been done in *that* situation to maintain or create peace?

Study groups could also have a Bible study on the topic of peace, or explore the theme through any of the other methods outlined in Chapter 6. Further Reading: Useful group material which is easily adapted to most groups, is *The Woodcraft Way – Peace* (The Woodcraft Folk, 13 Ritherdon Road, London SW17 8QE, 1982). Also useful: *The Peace Pack* (New Internationalist Publications, 42 Hythe Bridge Street, Oxford OX1 2EP); *The Nuclear Age*

(Christian Education Movement). Young people will doubt-less be moved by the cartoon book: *When the Wind Blows*, Raymond Briggs (Penguin Books, 1983).

Counselling
The need for young people to know where they can find both formal and informal counselling has been mentioned a number of times in this book.

Training in formal counselling can be had from various agencies: the diocesan adult education department should know suitable ones.

Every youth worker will realize the need to have some skills in informal counselling, for it is to him that young people are likely to turn for help. It is beyond the scope of this book to deal fully with the subject, except to list five important maxims: 1. always listen carefully (you may be able to do no more than this, but in itself it could be a great help); 2. never be judgemental; 3. try to help the young person find the answer to his own problem rather than tell him what to do; 4. keep confidential matters strictly confidential; 5. always refer cases which require specialist help.

Further reading: *A Handbook of Pastoral Counselling*, Peter G. Liddell (Mowbray 1983); *Still Small Voice*, Michael Jacobs (SPCK 1982); *Counselling Young People*, Tom Wylie (National Youth Bureau 1980).

Appendix 1

Resources – People

Virtually every diocese has at least one person with special responsibility for work with young people. Usually called the Diocesan Youth Officer, he or she is available to help with specific problems within the club or parish. Some are clergy with a special interest in youth work, others are lay people, more often than not trained professionals in youth matters. Both have at least some freedom from everyday parish and club activities to keep abreast of current thinking and can bring to a particular situation insights from elsewhere in the diocese and beyond. They can assist with the establishment of new ventures or are useful as outside 'consultants' when an assessment of existing work is required. Normally they keep lists of resources and may even have a stock of books, slides, films and tapes which can be borrowed or perused. Also, through their daily work they build up a network of contacts in other youth organizations and will match the needs of a group to available resources.

Training is another important part of a Diocesan Youth Officer's work. The value of training has been emphasized elsewhere. If not offering a course to meet the needs of a particular enquirer he should know of alternative agencies which will help. Other denominations such as the Roman Catholics, the Methodists and the United Reformed Church have Youth Officers too and produce very valuable teaching material. Contact can be made through a local minister; alternatively the Diocesan Youth Officer should know names and addresses.

Various other Christian organizations – e.g. British Council of Churches, Christian Aid and a number of Missionary Societies – also employ Youth Officers. They are particularly valuable in supplying resource material in specialist areas.

Appendix 2

Resources – Local Education Authorities

Local Education Authorities vary enormously in their generosity to voluntary organizations, usually in direct proportion to the importance they attach to youth work as a whole. Many LEAs are, however, generous in the financial aid they will give to church youth work, normally providing the provision is open to all young people in the area and not just to the church-going ones.

As it is the largest, I use the Inner London Education Authority as an example; exactly what is available in your area will need investigation – a visit to the youth office or a written enquiry will normally elicit the information required. Within ILEA the basic requirement is that a club (or project) is registered with the Authority. Naturally no LEA will give away money unless the recipient group meets certain requirements. There must be an adult committee responsible for the work, reasonably kept accounts of income and expenditure and competent staff to supervise activities (not necessarily trained or professionally qualified, but adults who can keep control and provide an interesting pro-gramme). This is no more than should be expected of any club or project and will constitute a threat only to organizations so incompetent as to deserve censure.

Once registered, applications can be made for grant aid. A portion (usually 50 per cent) of expenditure on rent, rates, heating, lighting and repair and redecoration can be claimed. Money is also available towards the cost of equipment. Larger groups can negotiate for staff payment too.

As well as financial help, the LEAs employ qualified personnel as Youth Officers who are willing to share their expertise with even the smallest club.

Such largesse is distributed on the basis of the recognized

fact that for every £1 contributed by an LEA toward voluntary work, about £10 of work is actually done. It obviously makes sense to be generous to voluntary groups, for if such groups were not functioning then the Authority would have to meet the total bill themselves or, perhaps more likely, no youth provision would exist at all. Some comment about not looking gift-horses in the mouth might be appropriate here! I repeat, though, that generosity and the exact conditions vary from one LEA to another.

Appendix 3

Sources of Teaching Material

First a word of warning. A well-equipped club does not necessarily make for good youth provision, neither is a 'teacher' good simply because he has access to endless resources. Having a wide selection of teaching material is only half the battle; the other half is knowing how to use it effectively. In fact the experienced person will learn to draw on all kinds of everyday objects and experiences to enliven his teaching and will always be concerned to adapt commercially produced resources to meet the precise needs of his group. After all, those who produce teaching aids do not know your particular group, only you can know exactly what their needs are.

Numerous resource centres are spread throughout Britain. The Diocesan Youth Officer should be able to supply addresses. Also many Christian bookshops have been established recently. They repay an occasional hour of browsing. Two resource centres deserve special mention: the National Society runs Religious Education Development Centres in York (at the College of Ripon and York St John, Lord Mayor's Walk, York YO3 7EX) and London (23 Kensington Square, London W8 5HN). Both are open to the public and will even open specially for parish groups out of normal hours. They have the widest and most up-to-date selection of books, posters, and visual aids. These are not for sale, but armed with the necessary information it is an easy matter to place an order with the publishers or through a local shop. The centres have extremely efficient staff who know all the latest material and are skilled in the techniques required to use them well.

Below are some useful sources of teaching material; addresses not listed can be found in Appendix 5.

Religious Education

Bible Reading Fellowship, St Michael's House, 2 Elizabeth Street, London SW1V 9RQ

Bible Society, 146 Queen Victoria Street, London EC4V 4BX

Christian Education Movement

Church Information Office, Church House, Dean's Yard, London SW1P 3NZ

Church Army, Winchester House, Independents Road, London SE3

Falcon/CPAS, Falcon Court, 32 Fleet Street, London EC4Y 1DB

Mothers' Union, 24 Tufton Street, London SW1P 3RB

National Christian Education Council, Robert Denholm House, Nutfield, Redhill, Surrey RH1 4HN

Teaching material by other publishers is available through bookshops.

Health Education

British Medical Association, BMA House, Tavistock Square, London WC1

Family Planning Association (Education Unit), 27–35 Mortimer Street, London W1N 7RJ

Health Education Council, 78 New Oxford Street, London WC1A 1AH

Institute for the Study of Drug Dependence, 3 Blackburn Road, London NW6 1XA

Release, 1 Elgin Avenue, London W9 3PR.
  Drug abuse information and help.

TACADE Publications Dept., 2 Mount Street, Manchester M2 5NG.
  Alcohol, drugs, smoking.

Community Awareness and Service

Community Service Volunteers

Help the Aged

Shelter, National Campaign for the Homeless, 157 Waterloo Road, London SE1 8UU

The Conservation Trust, 246 London Road, Earley, Reading RG6 1AJ

Race

Commission for Racial Equality, Elliot House, 10/12 Allington Street, London SW1E 5EH

Social Education

Macmillan Education Ltd, Houndmills, Basingstoke, Hants RG21 2YS; Showroom: 6 Little Essex Street, London WC2

Society for Academic Gaming and Simulation in Education and Training, Centre for Extension Studies, University of Technology, Loughborough LE11 3TU

Thomas Nelson & Sons Ltd, Lincoln Way, Windmill Road, Sunbury-on-Thames, Middx

Third World

Christian Aid

Church Missionary Society

Council for Education in World Citizenship, 42 Russell Square, London WC1

Oxfam

United Society for the Propagation of the Gospel

The following are sources of visual material on a number of topics:

Concord Film Council Ltd, 201 Felixstowe Road, Ipswich IP3 9BJ

CTVC Film Library, Walton Road, Bushey, Watford WD2 2JF

Educational Foundation for Visual Aids, Paxton House, Gipsy Road, London SE27 9SR

Rank Film Library, PO Box 20, Great West Road, Brentford TW8 9HR

Scottish Central Film Library, Dowanhill, 74 Victoria Crescent Road, Glasgow G12 9NJ

AVA Magazine, published three times a year, reviews recent visual aids and audio material suitable for church and educational use. Details of subscriptions from: Subscriptions Secretary, AVA Magazine, 1 Briarswood, Springfield, Chelmsford, Essex CM1 5UH.

Appendix 4

Books for Further Reading

Most books can be obtained from booksellers; those published by the National Youth Bureau, NAYC, General Synod Board of Education and the British Council of Churches can be ordered direct (addresses in Appendix 5).

General
Experience and Participation, Report of the Review Group on the Youth Service in England (HMSO, October 1982)
Kids at the Door, Bob Holman (Basil Blackwell, 1981)
A very readable and informative account of one man's experience with young people on a housing estate.

Youth Work Periodicals
Youth in Society (National Youth Bureau) monthly magazine.
Scene (National Youth Bureau) monthly newspaper.
Youth and Policy quarterly journal, includes fairly academic articles and a synopsis of parliamentary and press references to young people (The Editor, 'Burnbrae', Black Lane, Blaydon Burn, Blaydon, Tyne & Wear NE21 6DS).

Chapter 1 Young People and the Church Today
Youth in the Local Church, Fred Milson (National Youth Bureau, 1981)
Adolescence – Generation Under Pressure, John Conger (Harper and Row, 1979)
Towards a Church of England Policy for Work with Young People (General Synod Board of Education, 1980)
Young People and the Church (British Council of Churches, 1981)

Chapter 2 Leadership and Styles of Work

HELP! Finding and Keeping Volunteers for the Youth Club, Warren Redman (NAYC Publications, 1981)

Framework for the Recruitment, Training and Support of the Part-time Youth Worker, Michael Day (Brunel Institute of Organization & Social Studies, Brunel University, Uxbridge, Middlesex UB8 3PH)

Starting Out in Detached Work, Alan Rogers (NAYC Publications, 1981)

Starting Blocks, aspects of social education group work with young people, Dave Burley (National Youth Bureau, 1982)

Organize! A guide to practical politics for youth and community groups, Mark Smith (NAYC Publications, 1981)

The Politics of Youth Clubs, Sidney Bunt and Rob Gargrave (National Youth Bureau, 1980)

Why am I a Youth Worker? Fred Milson (National Association of Youth Clubs, 1972)

Creators not Consumers, Rediscovering Social Education, Mark Smith (NAYC Publications, 1982)

6 Training Sessions for Your Youth Work Team, Lyman Coleman and Denny Rydberg (Scripture Union, 1983)

Chapter 3 Management Committees and Support Groups

Talk about Management, A series of booklets about managing community-based agencies (National Youth Bureau, 1982)

Points of Order (Committees and meetings ... how they work), Janet Hunt (National Association of Youth Clubs, reprinted 1981)

Chapter 4 Running a Club

Clubs, Ken Webb (National Association of Youth Clubs, 1976)

For the Part-time Youth Worker, Nancy Lakeman and Charles Connelly (National Association of Youth Clubs, 1974)

The Youth Games Book, 1980, and *The Youth Arts and Craft*

Book, 1982, both by Alan Dearling and Howard Armstrong (Intermediate Treatment Resource Centre, Quarrier's Homes, Bridge of Weir, Renfrewshire PA11 3SA)

Chapter 5 Worship and Young People

All Generations, a handbook for Leaders of Family Worship (CIO, 1980)

Share the Word; Live, Learn and Worship; This is the Life, all by The Wadderton Group (CIO). Outline material for use with all ages.

Services for Special Occasions, Lawrence Jackson (Mowbray, 1982). Includes service for an All-Night Young People's Vigil and a Reunion Service for those who have been confirmed.

Words for Worship, Campling and Davis (Edward Arnold, reprinted 1982)

Praying Together in Word and Song, Taizé (English edition, Mowbray, 1982)

Hymn Books

Cry Hosanna, Fresh Sounds, Sounds of Living Water (all published by Hodder and Stoughton)

Jesus Praise (Scripture Union)

Psalm Praise (Falcon Books)

Music from Taizé (Collins)

Prayer Books for Young People

Praise, Prayers from Taizé (Mowbray, 1977)

Living Words, With Open Heart (Gill and Macmillan) and other books by Michel Quoist

A Diary of Private Prayer, John Baillie (Oxford). First printed 1936 but still valued by some older young people.

More Prayers for Young People, William Barclay (Fount Paperbacks, 1977)

Lord of the Morning, Lord of Life, etc., Frank Topping

(Lutterworth) Half a dozen or more illustrated books of prayer.

You must be Joking Lord (Mayhew McCrimmon, 1975) and other books by Michael Hollings and Etta Gullick.

Chapter 6 Confirmation and Spiritual Growth

Crisis for Confirmation, edited by Michael Perry (SCM, 1967). Out of print, but a collection of essays worth reading.

Partners in Learning, A church community education programme. Annually produced material for all ages. (Methodist Church Division of Education & Youth/ National Christian Education Council)

Using the Bible, a series of booklets about using the Bible with young people, in drama, etc. (Bible Society)

Alive in God's World – Handbook for Leaders of 13–15 year olds, The Wadderton Group (CIO, 1970)

Experiments in Prayer and *Experiments in Growth*, Betsy Caprio (Ave Maria Press, 1973, 1976). Over 70 'experiments' which (with some adaptation) are valuable activities for use with study groups.

Serendipity, Youth Bible Study Series. Leaders' Guide and various student books (Scripture Union, 1983)

Educational Games

Eight Games for Group Leaders, Martin Goodlad and Eric Whitton (Methodist Church Division of Education & Youth/General Synod Board of Education, 1981)

Gamesters Handbook, Donna Bandes and Howard Phillips (Hutchinson & Co, 24 Highbury Crescent, London N5 11RX)

Confirmation Courses

A far fuller list (which includes resources on a whole range of Christian teaching topics), *Making Ready – A review of training and resource material*, is available from The Bristol Diocesan Education Department, Church House, 23 Great George Street, Bristol BS1 5QZ.

Confirmation Cook Book, A compendium of outlines for a flexible training course in the Christian Faith. Written by the Winchester Diocesan Education Team. (Mowbray, 1980). Highly recommended for its variety and imagination. Easily adapted to groups of different ages and ability. Encourages *experience* as well as the learning of facts.

My Confirmation Notebook, Hugh Montefiore (SPCK, 1968). Adult language, but useful source on major theological topics.

Going Firm, Andrew Knowles (Falcon, Audio-Visual, 1979). Cassette tape and worksheets. Enough material for ten interesting sessions for the over-12s.

Not in Front of the Children, Ron Green (Mowbray, 1980). Teaching material on basic Christian topics for use over two years or more with 12-15 year olds.

Chapter 8 Residential Events
Catering for Residential Events (Inter-School Christian Fellowship. Available through Scripture Union)

Appendix 5

Addresses

Denominational Headquarters Organizations
General Synod Board of Education, Church House, Dean's Yard, London SW1P 3NZ
Tel. 01 222 9011
Baptist Union of Great Britain and Ireland, Baptist Church House, 4 Southampton Row, London WC1B 4AB
Tel. 01 405 9803
Catholic Youth Service Council, 41 Cromwell Road, London SW7 2DH
Tel. 01 589 7550
Methodist Association of Youth Clubs, 2 Chester House, Pages Lane, London N10 1PR
Tel. 01 444 9845
Salvation Army, 101 Queen Victoria Street, London EC4P 4EP
Tel. 01 236 5222
United Reformed Church, 86 Tavistock Place, London WC1H 9RT
Tel. 01 837 7661
British Council of Churches (*Youth Unit*), 2 Eaton Gate, London SW1W 9BL
Tel. 01 730 9611

Christian Youth Organizations
Boys' Brigade, Brigade House, Parsons Green, London SW6 4TH
Tel. 01 736 8481

Campaigners, Campaigners' House, St Mark's Close, Colney Heath, St Albans, Herts AL4 0NQ
Tel. Bowmansgreen 23063

Christian Education Movement, 2 Chester House, Pages Lane, London N10 1PR
Tel. 01 444 8383

CYFA (Christian Youth Fellowship Association), 32 Fleet Street, London EC4Y 1DB
Tel. 01 353 0751

Church Army Youth Service, GSC House, North Circular Road, London NW10 7UG
Tel. 01 903 3736

Church Lads' and Church Girls' Brigade, Claude Hardy House, 15 Etchingham Park Road, London N3 2DU
Tel. 01 349 2616

Covenanter Union, Nasmith House, 175 Tower Bridge Road, London SE1 2AG
Tel. 01 407 4985

Frontier Youth Trust, 130 City Road, London EC1V 2NJ
Tel. 01 250 1966

Girl Guides Association, 17–19 Buckingham Palace Road, London SW1W 0PT
Tel. 01 834 6242

Girls' Brigade National Church for England and Wales, Brigade House, Parsons Green, London SW6 4TH
Tel. 01 736 8461

Girls Friendly Society, Townsend House, 126 Queen's Gate, London SW7 5LQ
Tel. 01 589 9628

Royal School of Church Music, Addington Palace, Croydon CR9 5AD
Tel. 01 654 7676

Scout Association, Baden-Powell House, Queen's Gate, London SW7 5JS
Tel. 01 584 7030

Scripture Union, 130 City Road, London EC1V 2NJ
Tel. 01 250 1966

Some 'Secular' Youth Organizations
Duke of Edinburgh's Award Scheme, 5 Prince of Wales
Terrace, London W8 5PG
Tel. 01 937 5205
National Association for Asian Youth, 46 High Street,
Southall, Middlesex
Tel. 01 574 1325
National Association of Boys' Clubs, 24 Highbury Grove,
London N5 2EA
Tel. 01 359 9281
National Association of Youth Clubs, 30 Peacock Lane,
Leicester LE1 5NY
Tel. 0533 29514
National Council for Voluntary Youth Services, 26 Bedford
Square, London WC1B 3HU
Tel. 01 636 4066
National Trust (Junior Division), The Old Grape House,
Clivedon, Taplow, Maidenhead, Berks SL6 0HZ
Tel. 062 86 4228
National Youth Bureau, 17–23 Albion Street, Leicester
LE1 6GD
Tel. 0533 554775

Charities and Missions with Youth Departments
Christian Aid, 240 Ferndale Road, London SW9
Tel. 01 733 5500
Church Missionary Society, 157 Waterloo Road, London
SE1 8UU
Tel. 01 928 8681
Help the Aged, Education Dept, 318 St Paul's Road, London
N1
Tel. 01 359 6316
Oxfam, 274 Banbury Road, Oxford OX2 7DZ
Tel. 0865 56777
Save the Children Fund, Mary Datchelor House, Camberwell
Grove, London SE5
Tel. 01 703 5400

United Society for the Propagation of the Gospel, 15 Tufton Street, London SW1P 3QQ
Tel. 01 222 4222

Volunteer Projects
The following organizations provide volunteer posts for young people.
Careforce, 130 City Road, London EC1V 2NJ. Tel. 01 250 1966. Evangelical.
Christians Abroad, 15 Tufton Street, London SW1P 3QQ. Tel. 01 222 2165. Mainly skilled posts.
Community Service Volunteers, 237 Pentonville Road, London N1 9NJ
Tel. 01 278 6601
International Voluntary Service, 'Ceresole House', 53 Regent Road, Leicester LE1 6YL
Tel. 0533 541862
Root Groups, organized by USPG (see address above). Year-long placements for young people in small Christian communities.
Time for God, 2 Chester House, Pages Lane, London N10 1PR.
Tel. 01 883 1504. Ecumenical.

For suppliers of films and other teaching material see Appendix 3.

Notes

Chapter 2 Leadership and Styles of Work

1. from: *Framework for the Recruitment, Training and Support of the Part-time Youth Worker*, Michael Day p. 7. Brunel Institute of Organization and Social Studies, 1982.
2. *Op. cit.* p. 6.
3. *Experience and Participation*. Report of the Review Group on the Youth Service in England (HMSO, 1982). See especially pp. 19–25.
4. Quoted in *The Politics of Youth Clubs*, Sidney Bunt and Ron Gargrave, p. 63. National Youth Bureau, 1980.
5. *Experience and Participation*, p. 34.
6. *Youth in the Local Church*, Fred Milson, p. 2 (National Youth Bureau, 1981).
7. *The Politics of Youth Clubs*, p. 146.

Chapter 3 Management Committees and Support Groups

1. *Experience and Participation*, p. 74.

Chapter 4 Running a Club

1. For useful details on the relevant law see also: Chapter 9 of *Clubs*, by Ken Webb (National Association of Youth Clubs, 1976).
2. The Politics of Youth Clubs, p. 65f.
3. By Hugh Warner (SCM Press Ltd)

Chapter 5 Worship and Young People

1. In writing this chapter I am particularly indebted to two books: *Learning through Liturgy*, Gwen Kennedy Neville

and John M. Westerhoff III. (The Seabury Press, New York, 1978). *Worship and the Child*, edited by Ronald C. D. Jasper (SPCK, 1975).

Books for further reading are listed in Appendix 4.

Index